Van Gogh's Gardens

van gogh's

Derek Fell

GARDENS

SIMON & SCHUSTER

NEW YORK LONDON TORONTO SYDNEY SINGAPORE

SIMON & SCHUSTER
Rockefeller Center
1230 Avenue of the Americas
New York, NY 10020

Copyright © 2001 by Derek Fell
All rights reserved, including the right of
reproduction in whole or in part in any form.

SIMON & SCHUSTER and colophon are
registered trademarks of Simon & Schuster, Inc.

Designed by Jim Wageman, Wigwag

Manufactured in the United States of America
10   9   8   7   6   5   4   3   2   1

Library of Congress Cataloging-in-Publication
Data is available.

ISBN 0-7432-0233-3

All photographs by Derek Fell, except:
Kröller-Müller Museum, Otterlo: pages 2, 62, 64–
65, 82–83, 86, 96–97, 130–31, 141, 152; Van Gogh
Museum, Amsterdam: pages 5, 98, 163; The J. Paul
Getty Museum, Los Angeles: pages 7, 159; Bridgeman
Art Library, New York: pages 15, 27, 29, 30–31, 33,
49, 106–7, 108–9, 133, 134–35, 166–67, 175;
Erich Lessing/Art Resource, NY: pages 41, 79, 99,
187; Cincinnati Art Museum: pages 46–47, 56–57,
124; The Art Institute of Chicago: pages 61, 115;
The Rudolf Staechelin Family Foundation, Basel: pages
78, 88–89, 91; Kunstahaus Zurich: pages 103, 104;
The Minneapolis Institute of Art: pages 113, 145, 171;
Peter Willi/Bridgeman Art Library: page 149

Photo research by Naomi Ben-Shahar

FRONTISPIECE
*Vincent van Gogh,
Pine Trees and
Dandelions in the
Garden of Saint-Paul
Hospital, detail.*

OPPOSITE
*Vincent van Gogh,
Self-Portrait with
Pipe and Straw
Hat, 1888. Van Gogh
Museum, Amsterdam.*

a c k n o w l e d g m e n t s

I value the support of my wife, Carolyn, who helped me interpret van Gogh's gardening philosophy. She accompanied me not only to his resting place at Auvers-sur-Oise, in France, but also to the Van Gogh Museum in Amsterdam and the Kröller-Müller State Museum, near Otterlo, in Holland. She also reviewed my conclusions in the light of her training as a color specialist. An expert floral arranger, Carolyn was responsible for creating the several floral still lifes featured in this book.

Wendy Fields, my grounds supervisor, helped to plant many of the colorful example plantings featured in the photography, while Kathy Nelson and Joan Haas helped me organize my extensive file library. Among garden owners, I wish to thank Princess Greta Sturtza, of Normandy, France; Mary Mallet, also of Normandy; and Timothy and Isabelle Vaughan, of Brittany, France.

Special thanks also to Olive Dunn, a retired florist and garden writer living in Invercargill, New Zealand. Olive's cottage garden features many ideas inspired by Impressionist painters, and when she learned of my intention to create a "Van Gogh Garden" featuring orange and black as the principal components, she planted one herself and wrote about its success in *The New Zealand Gardener*. When I learned of her enthusiasm for the Van Gogh Garden and the compliments she received from visitors, I traveled with Carolyn to Invercargill and photographed her garden for this book.

I am fortunate to have as a neighbor Dr. Theodore R. Monica, Jr., professor of art history at Bucks County Community College, who is an authority on modern art with a special interest in the Impressionists. At various times during my research into van Gogh's art and lifestyle, he willingly provided me with the benefit of his expertise and opinions.

Finally, I am indebted to my literary agent, Albert Zuckerman, who helped me organize my initial thoughts with a wealth of good suggestions; also Constance Herndon, my editor, who recognized the need for the book and brought to bear a team of talented people at Simon & Schuster. Designer Jim Wageman has brought this material to light in a way I never thought possible. My thanks as well to Stephen Motika and Linda Evans for their hard work.

Vincent Van Gogh, Irises, 1889. The J. Paul Getty Museum, Los Angeles.

contents

preface

"I am very busy gardening and have sown a little garden full of poppies, sweet peas, and mignonette. Now we must wait and see what becomes of it."
Letter to Theo, from his London lodgings
(April 1874)

O<small>F ALL THE PAINTINGS</small> made by Vincent van Gogh over a career that spanned only ten years, his images of flowers and gardens project his extraordinary energy and unique interpretations of nature. The sunflower series, the irises, the cutting gardens of Provence, his series of floral bouquets while living in Paris, all are images that remain indelible in our minds among his tremendous outpouring of work.

As I researched van Gogh's garden philosophy through his letters and paintings, one passage stood out as an example of the childlike delight he took in exploring gardens. To his brother Theo, he confided his joy: "I have come back from a day at Montmajour. . . . We explored the old garden together and stole some excellent figs. If it had been bigger it would have made me think of Zola's Paradou—green reeds, vines, ivy, fig trees, olives, pomegranates with lusty flowers of the brightest orange, hundred-year-old cypresses, ash trees and willows, rock oaks, half-broken flights of steps, ogive windows in ruins, blocks of white rocks covered in lichen, and scattered fragments of crumbling walls here and there among the green."

When van Gogh closed the final chapter of his life, he left not only a legacy of incredible paintings but also hundreds of pages of letters that offer insights into his art, as no other artist has done before or since. His observations of nature, his theories about color harmonies, and his choice of garden motifs allow us to understand clearly what impressed and inspired him about cultivated spaces. On a more practical note, these letters—often written deliberately to teach and instruct—can help us become better gardeners. Indeed, knowing what this great artist liked about plants and gardens has helped me create a series of twenty unusual theme gardens at my own home, Cedaridge Farm, in rural Pennsylvania. I am happy to share some of the lessons learned from Vincent van Gogh, and to show how my wife and I have made our property infinitely more beautiful from the experience.

Presented throughout this book are specific planting ideas and garden designs inspired by van Gogh's art—not only designs based on his favorite color harmonies, many accomplished in small areas, but also complete garden spaces, such as vegetable gardens, cutting gardens, shade gardens, and skyline effects using the trees and shrubs he painted. I've included tips concerning specific plants that van Gogh admired—for example, how to delay the wilting of sunflowers, which he found frustrating; how to grow lavender to perfection; and how to time the seeding of poppies so they provide a succession of color from early spring through autumn.

I hope that, after seeing the evocative paintings, evaluating the hundred or so specific gardening ideas he expressed a special fondness for, and seeing these ideas interpreted in a modern context, other home gardeners will be inspired to create beautiful, uplifting, spiritual spaces.

Van Gogh's Gardens

van gogh's
LOVE OF
GARDENS

"*MacKnight came again yesterday to see me . . .
and said that he liked my garden.*"

Letter to Theo, explaining a friend's response to
his painting of a cutting garden (August 1888)

A *field of sunflowers near Arles,
in the countryside of Provence,
where van Gogh painted a series
of sunflower still life arrangements
to commemorate the arrival of his
friend Paul Gauguin.*

VINCENT VAN GOGH, one of the world's most admired painters, was passionate about gardens and gardening. He cultivated a small garden with cottage annuals at a rental property when he worked as an art dealer and teacher in London, planting seeds of poppies, sweet peas, and mignonette. Later, when he took up painting, he featured flowers and gardens prominently in his art and used them repeatedly as a metaphor to describe his artistic technique and his feelings about life. He retained a strong affection for his father's parsonage garden in Holland, and when he fell under the spell of Impressionism, he wrote enthusiastically about many other gardens he encountered during his ten productive years as an artist. These include the Arles hospital garden; a Provençal farm garden near Arles; the Garden of the Poets in Arles; the walled garden of the Asylum of Saint-Paul; Dr. Paul Gachet's flower garden at Auvers; and the artist Charles Daubigny's rose garden at Auvers. All are featured prominently in his paintings and are referred to enthusiastically in his letters.

Floral still lifes of sunflowers were as dear to him as waterlilies were to Monet and roses to Renoir. But as beloved as Monet and Renoir are today, it is van Gogh's paintings that command record prices at auction—$8.4 million for a simple sketch entitled *Garden of Flowers* (1888), almost $54 million for *Irises* (1889), $39 million for *Vase with Sunflowers* (1889), and $82.5 million for his 1890 *Portrait of Dr. Gachet,* which shows him holding a foxglove to symbolize his medical profession.

Unlike Monet and Renoir, van Gogh was unable to gain financial success from his art. Both of his contemporaries gained artistic claim and financial success in midlife and were able to develop ambitious gardens, which they used in their paintings (Monet at Giverny, near Paris, and Renoir at Les Collettes,

near Nice), but van Gogh remained far too poor. Still, while Monet and Renoir wrote little about their gardening philosophies, van Gogh wrote reams describing his responses to the gardens he painted. His letters are filled with gardening ideas, many of them written to his younger brother Theo, who provided financial assistance. He also wrote at length to his younger sister Wilhelmien. Indeed, it is in his tender letters to her that he articulated many of his best planting schemes, suggesting she try them out in the family garden. In those letters van Gogh suggested color harmonies and the plants she should grow to achieve them. He even expressed the notion that his planting theories could fill a book. Indeed they can!

While van Gogh claimed the sunflower as his own, he also heaped praise on many other kinds of plants—especially red poppies, grasses, and irises. His choice of floral motifs often reflected his mood— ghostly white-hooded arums during bouts of depression; flowering shrubs such as vibrant pink oleanders when he was upbeat; and trees such as dark green spirelike cypresses writhing with energy and contorted olive trees vibrant with silvery leaves when he was feeling a sense of inner turmoil. He imagined trees with near-human characteristics, describing a noble pine with a trunk scarred by lightning as a once proud man stricken by a heart attack.

Van Gogh's first garden subject as a painter was entitled *Bulb Fields* (1883). Showing a bulb merchant's production plots planted with rectangles of blue, yellow, pink, and red hyacinths, it is an example of the artist's fascination with strong lines of perspective. Two years later he captured scenes of his father's walled parsonage garden at Nuenen in Holland, painted through all the seasons. One shows the garden covered in snow, emphasizing strong lines of perspective created by the walls of the garden and those of its neighbors. In the background a dark

church tower rises from the flat landscape against a lemon sky, the ornate structure creating a distant focal point like a garden gazebo.

Another painting of the parsonage garden shows a person shoveling snow from a path beneath orchard trees that outline sinuous silhouettes against a wintry

A *recurring theme in van Gogh's work is thatched cottages, first painted in Holland and then in France. These cozy cottages are located at Saintes-Maries-de-la-Mer, a fishing village on the shores of the Mediterranean, where he painted an entire street of thatched cottages with small garden plots featuring spiky yuccas and red geraniums.*

lowing chestnut trees in the environs of Paris and massive sycamores lining village streets in Provence.

When van Gogh moved to Auvers-sur-Oise, north of Paris, in the last months of his life, he wrote how pleased he was to see cottages still roofed in thatch, for they were disappearing in the French

sky; yet another is autumnal, showing a pond and small boat dock. From the garden van Gogh harvested baskets of fruits and vegetables and found birds' nests to paint. In the surrounding landscape he was drawn to gnarled, pollarded willows and avenues of pencil-straight poplars creating majestic architectural lines like the nave of a cathedral. These natural elements became etched in his memory as reminders of home. Indeed, in his erratic journey through life, he found trees to be particularly inspirational forces—including bil-

countryside. Throughout his travels in Holland and France, thatched cottages and their gardens were a favorite motif, as though he hungered for a little home of his own and he perceived thatch as a metaphor for a nest. Thatch remained an appealing feature of structures he painted throughout his life— farmhouses in the countryside of Holland, fishermen's cottages in the Camargue on the Mediterranean, as well as rural cottages with front gardens in the agricultural community of Auvers, where he spent his last days tormented by perceptions of failure and fears of being a burden to his brother.

Many of van Gogh's early images are dark and gloomy. He was living in troubled circumstances, having failed at relationships with women and in several career moves that included dealing in art, teaching, and missionary work. His somber palette did not lighten until he moved to Paris, where he came under the influence of works by Pissarro, Monet, Manet, Cézanne, and Renoir.

THE INFLUENCE OF IMPRESSIONISM

Moving to Paris to pursue a painting career, van Gogh settled in Montmartre, where he shared an apartment with Theo. There he discovered the Impressionists, who met in local cafés and restaurants to discuss painting technique. Van Gogh's letters contain detailed references to the Impressionist movement and his admiration for the paintings. Before his brother joined him in Paris, he wrote: "There is much to see here. . . . In Antwerp I did not even know what Impressionists were; now I have seen them, and though *not* being one of the club yet, I have much admired certain Impressionists' pictures—*Degas,* nude figure—*Claude Monet,* landscape."

Though van Gogh embraced the Impressionists, and exhibited at their independent exhibitions, he did not like to be labeled an Impressionist. He saw the movement as a stepping-stone in his own artistic development, as he expressed in a letter to Theo: "I remain among the Impressionists because it professes nothing, and binds you to nothing, and as one of the comrades I need not declare my formula."

The Impressionists liked to paint outdoors—*en plein air*—to capture fleeting moments of light, especially in landscapes. The recent invention of oil paints in tubes was key in allowing them to work outdoors. Typically, they applied paint quickly and spontaneously to capture such atmospheric conditions as misty mornings, rainy streets, snow-covered gardens, and even wind blowing through foliage. They used dabs and dots of color applied in thin layers to project unusually colorful, evanescent visual sensations.

During his two-year stay in Montmartre, van Gogh associated with the Impressionists and vigorously championed their cause, telling his sister: "The dreary schoolmasters now on the Salon jury will not even admit the Impressionists. Not that the latter will be so intent on having the doors opened; they will put on their own exhibition. If you now bear in mind that by then I want to have at least fifty paintings ready."

Although feeling and expression are evident in most Impressionist art, it is van Gogh's intensity that set him apart from the other Impressionists. For the times his bold, impetuous, energetic style was too big a departure from prevailing artistic tastes. Though Monet's and Renoir's work was at first ridiculed, it presented softer, more romantic imagery, which gradually gained acceptance because it was easier to appreciate. Their innovative painting style is characterized by swift, comma-shaped brushstrokes of color and an ability to capture shimmering, vibrant sensations of sunlight and shadow. At an exhibition of Impressionist work that included some of van Gogh's paintings, both Gauguin and Monet acknowledged that their Dutch colleague's work was the best.

But van Gogh's interests in and use of color went well beyond those of other Impressionists, and he eventually declared a separation from the movement. He pursued his own unique technique—one more expressive in its response to nature than that of any of the other Impressionists, including Monet. Impressionism was the art movement that most strongly informed his ideas, but with his fiercely independent style of artistic expression, van Gogh left Impressionism behind.

The lavender in this field in Provence, grown for lavender oil, is similar to one van Gogh painted at the coastal resort of Saintes-Maries-de-la-Mer. He liked to discover large expanses of a dominant color like this— orange wheat fields, blood red poppies, and yellow buttercups.

THE INFLUENCE OF PARIS
AND THE FRENCH COUNTRYSIDE

A hilly rural community overlooking the city, Montmartre was crowned with windmills that ground orrisroot into a fixative used in perfumes. Some had been converted into restaurants and open-air dance halls that were thronged with young Parisians in the evenings and on weekend afternoons. Van Gogh's focus was not on the vitality of the revelers that so attracted Renoir but on the remnants of country gardens that were fast giving way to the sprawl of city

RIGHT

Lilac, apple blossom, and yellow kerria bloom simultaneously in the garden of the Asylum of Saint-Paul, where van Gogh painted several groves of lilacs.

development. Surrounding the crest of Montmartre were bountiful vegetable gardens that supplied the Paris markets. Here the plots were fenced in to provide security and separation, the vegetables forming blocks like the production plots of Dutch bulb farms. The blocks of spinach, lettuce, and cabbage formed a quilt pattern that provided van Gogh with the pronounced lines of perspective he loved to paint. Surrounding the mount, a labyrinth of quaint cobbled streets, restaurants, and dance halls formed a gather-

ing place for artists where new aesthetic concepts were hotly debated.

The markets of Montmartre and Paris were filled with fresh flowers, many rushed by train from France's cut-flower center near Nice. In the spring of 1887, when van Gogh took up the mantle of Impressionism, he threw himself into a frenzy of painting floral still lifes to brighten his palette and invited friends to bring him fresh flowers from their gardens. His letters contain meticulous detail about how the colorful flowers were experiments in color values— vases of red poppies against a dark blue background, orange crown imperials against a violet background, spiky red gladiolus and red zinnias in hot color groupings. An arrangement of dark maroon hollyhocks and white scabiosa represents a black and white color contrast.

As van Gogh wandered further afield, he painted apple green rowing boats floating on the blue River Seine, itself overhung with yellow willow leaves and grasses—a predominantly blue and yellow color harmony. As spring advanced, his canvases captured the parks of Paris erupting with groves of chestnut and lilac trees; meadows sparkling with blue cornflowers and red poppies; pastures carpeted with white daisies, blue vetch, and yellow coltsfoot. He found beauty in the undergrowth—not only woodlands speckled with wildflowers but paths where the fallen petals of a redbud tree colored the ground pink. He painted groves of slender trees standing on an evergreen carpet of English ivy, their dark, lustrous leaves contrasting with mottled bark coloration. Art historian

Van Gogh loved woodland paths in spring, carpeted with fallen petals such as those of the redbud tree. Here the ephemeral beauty of fallen rhododendron petals provides a dramatic contrast with black branches. In autumn he admired similar carpeting effects with orange poplar leaves and chestnut brown pine needles.

Van Gogh was allowed beyond the walls of the Asylum of Saint-Paul only in the company of a warden, but the countryside was diverse in its attractions, including deep woodlands and magnificent views of the Alpilles Mountains. He associated ivy-covered trees with his mental affliction—the ivy was a burden the tree might not relish but could survive.

Ingo F. Walther observed of this scene: "This green infinity with dabs of bright yellows and white is not a faithful copy of a wood. Yet the sense of growth fills the canvas all the more powerfully: there is a vitality in this burgeoning greenery."

Outside a restaurant van Gogh painted an arrangement of green Versailles-style planter boxes, each containing a tree, their color echoing the colors of the green shutters. Entitled *Exterior of a Restaurant at Asnières* (1887), the painting includes a flush of pink from a bush of oleander, but it is not floral beauty that has captured his fancy—it is the green of the planter boxes and shutters. He remembered the planter boxes later when he began decorating his rental property in Arles. Coincidentally, this is the same green Monet later chose to decorate the shut-

ters and garden furniture of his house and garden at Giverny and the same style of planter he used to grow tree fuchsias. His ideas about color combinations with plants dovetailed with van Gogh's. Both painters independently discovered the triad combination of red, green, and silver—Monet in a poppy field in the Normandy countryside (the silvery tones coming from wild sage) and van Gogh in a poppy field in Provence (the silvery tones coming from lavender foliage).

THE INFLUENCE OF JAPAN

After little more than a year in Paris, van Gogh found the city confining and yearned for a sunnier climate and a clear sky. Like the other Impressionists, he had fallen in love with Japanese painting and sought an environment that would allow him to explore that interest. "I believe that by looking at nature under a brighter sky, one might gain a truer idea of the Japanese way of feeling and drawing," he declared to Theo. In another letter explaining his liking for Arles, he remarked: "About this staying in the South, even if it is more expensive, consider: we like Japanese painting, we have felt its influence, all the Impressionists have that in common; then why not go to Japan, that is to say, the equivalent of Japan, the South?"

In a letter to his sister, his enthusiasm for Japanese art waxed poetic: "If we study Japanese art, we see a man who is undoubtedly wise, philosophical, and intelligent, who spends his time . . . studying a single blade of grass, and then the seasons, the wide aspects of the countryside, then animals, then the human figure . . . isn't it almost a true religion these simple Japanese teach us, who live in nature as though they themselves were flowers?"

Monet expressed almost the same sentiments about Japanese art when he declared that he admired most the Japanese artisan who could see a fragment to suggest a whole, and he repeated the story of a Japanese stonemason who placed a single rose in view each day to help him with his tedious task of building a wall.

In Paris van Gogh discovered the beauty of Japanese woodblock prints and started a collection that he mounted as an exhibition. He was captivated by the animated style of Japanese artists, marveling at the way a tempestuous sea is drawn with waves that resemble claws trying to sink a ship. He visited galleries specializing in Japanese art and copied Japanese prints.

In search of a landscape similar to that of Japan, he moved to the countryside of Provence, drawn there by descriptions of peasants who wore cone-shaped straw hats like Japanese farmworkers; fields enclosed by reed windbreaks resembling the bamboo fences of Japanese art; wheat fields and orchards laid out in a geometry resembling rice paddies, stretching to a horizon backed by high mountains; plum and peach trees with acutely angled branches and a brilliancy of blossoms like those painted by Japanese artists; and stone outcrops with pines twisted into weathered shapes like Japanese bonsai. In a letter to Theo, he declared: "All my work is in a way founded on Japanese art, and we do not know enough about Japanese prints. In decadence in its own country, pigeonholed in collections already impossible to find in Japan itself, Japanese art is taking root again among the French Impressionist artists."

Branches of blossoming peach in an angular display similar to that in Japanese woodblock prints van Gogh admired. He used orchard blossoms as inspiration for paintings of still life arrangements.

To Gauguin, in a letter eagerly anticipating his friend's move to Arles, van Gogh confided a special thrill: "There is still present in my mind the emotion produced by my own journey from Paris to Arles last winter. How I peered out to see whether it was like Japan yet! Childish, wasn't it?"

Van Gogh was not alone in his fascination with Japanese art and culture. Monet, too, found Japanese art full of interesting compositions and perspectives and amassed a collection that survives today in his restored home at Giverny, north of Paris. Other members of the Impressionist circle—Degas, Cassatt, Caillebotte, Gauguin, and Pissarro—all acknowledged the influence of Japanese art in their work.

Of particular importance to van Gogh was the choice of subject matter in Japanese art. Traditionally, artists wishing to impress the Paris salon judges chose grandiose themes, such as religious motifs, battle scenes, and expansive mountain landscapes. But under the influence of Japanese prints circulating around Paris, van Gogh selected evocative close-ups of plants, such as flowering almond branches; intimate garden spaces in all seasons; trees weathered into a sculptural beauty by wind and harsh soil; decorative structures such as carts, fountains, stone walls, and reed fences; and implements to work the land, such as wheelbarrows, wooden hay rakes, orchard ladders, and scythes.

Provence did not disappoint van Gogh. "I have found my Japan," he exclaimed. Most important, a clarity of light accentuated colors, creating a landscape far removed from the grime and frenetic pace of Paris.

Letters to Theo from this period are almost breathless with praise for the area around Arles, where he chose to spend two years. He first captured the countryside cloaked in a freak snowstorm, then bursting with blossoms from the successive flowering of the fruit orchards during a crisp, clear, warming

trend. For six weeks he painted orchard scenes, starting with almond blossoms in late February and ending with flowering pear trees in April. So intense was his passion that he usually completed a complicated canvas in a single day.

THE COTTAGE GARDENS

A parade of color followed the flowering orchards. The orchards were filled with poppies. Van Gogh found several cottage gardens to paint—mostly cutting gardens planted along dirt roads leading to farmsteads—and he was filled with so much enthusiasm for a garden of annuals that he wrote long explanations of its special appeal to Wilhelmien and Theo. He named the flowers (yellow marigolds, blue nigellas, and red zinnias in particular) and the background highlights (spirelike cypresses and contorted fig trees). Repeatedly he used the flowers to explain his theories on color harmonies, especially to Wil.

To Wil he wrote a long explanation of the significance of a painting entitled *Memory of the Garden at Etten* (1888), which depicts one of his father's parsonage gardens in Holland. He told Wil that the youngest of three figures in the painting is his depiction of her, the oldest figure his mother, and a third figure picking flowers a maidservant. He explained: "I know this is hardly what one might call a likeness, but for me it renders the poetic character and the style of the garden as I feel it. . . . I don't know whether you can understand that one may make a poem only by arranging colors in the same way that one can say comforting things in music." Significantly, the garden combined flowers and vegetables, divided into halves by a meandering gravel path—one side featuring a riot of yellow dahlias and red geraniums, the other plots of vegetables, notably cabbages.

As the year progressed, weeks went by without rainfall and the gardens became less verdant. Van Gogh lamented that he would find too few garden motifs to paint. At one point he even complained that the roses had finished blooming, and he praised a canvas painted by Renoir of a rose garden at Wargemont, on the Normandy coast. The roses of Renoir's canvas were in an island bed in front of a house, trained to a single stem with a topknot of leaves and flowers. The roses were underplanted with a carpet of flowering geraniums, the bed edged with violets, and van Gogh considered going to Nice "to find Renoir's rose gardens." (Twenty years later Renoir moved to Nice and established a home with a rose garden in the adjacent fishing village of Cagnes-sur-Mer.)

A TAPESTRY GARDEN

As cooler weather returned to Arles in autumn, van Gogh discovered the special qualities of a public garden facing his house. It was filled with trees and shrubs that presented a weave of subtle foliage contrasts, shapes, and textures—what landscape designers today call a tapestry garden. He described it as "a piece of garden with a weeping tree, cedar bushes shaped into balls, a bush of oleander . . . with a lemony sky above it all, and the colors now have the richness and intensity of autumn." He named it the Garden of the Poets because he imagined poets wandering along its gravel paths, inspired to compose poetry by the majesty of the trees. But when he painted it he changed its organization, leaving out plants that did not please him. "That's three times now I've painted the same spot," he wrote his brother.

When Gauguin arrived from Paris to visit van Gogh, he was welcomed by a series of sunflower still lifes specially painted to celebrate the event and to decorate their rooms. As the seasons advanced and temperatures dropped, the leaves of poplars and

grapevines changed, and van Gogh discovered new sensations of color. He saw how the russet colors of a vineyard were intensified after a light shower of rain, a setting sun turning them bright red; he saw how fallen leaves created a yellow carpet over bare ground, providing a beautiful contrast for the lighter

colored trunks of columnar poplars. Gauguin painted the same scene but chose a conventional view, at ground level, while van Gogh painted from a high elevation, as though in a tree, so the carpet of fallen leaves was prominent.

At first van Gogh described life with Gauguin as happy, the two of them sharing excursions into the countryside in search of stimulating subjects to paint. But they soon annoyed each other, and heated arguments ensued—over Vincent's messy habits and about

painting technique. Van Gogh admired Gauguin's work but suggested ways to improve his pictures. In particular he did not like Gauguin's flat application of color. Conversely, Gauguin believed his friend would be a better painter if he worked more from memory. The tensions and mental stress eventually caused van Gogh to threaten Gauguin with a razor, and in penance he cut off part of his right ear and took it to a local prostitute. Gauguin immediately left Arles for Paris; Theo immediately left Paris for Arles; and van Gogh was hospitalized in a state of physical and mental exhaustion, diagnosed with a mental condition that brings on seizures and severe bouts of melancholy.

Van Gogh returned to the hospital several times for treatment, but in the spring he celebrated an escape from depression by painting a vibrant courtyard garden in the hospital grounds. A formal garden in a cart-wheel design resembling a magnificent sunburst, it still exists with eight pie-shaped beds displaying early annuals and flowering bulbs. There was also a circular goldfish pond in the middle. Van Gogh noted the joyous, colorful aspects of his composition but imagined the garden with lurking demons—three tall serpentlike trees standing as sentinels at each corner and a line of somber boxwood on contorted trunks. He dashed off a preliminary sketch showing the garden with all its design elements, including lots of terra-cotta containers. Yet in his finished painting he excluded them, concentrating on the plants and spatial elements of the design. Then he wrote to Wil to explain details of the courtyard garden, identifying all the plants that impressed him—forget-me-nots, Christmas roses, anemones, ranunculuses, wallflowers, daisies, orange trees, and oleanders.

LEFT

Van Gogh liked the fall for its strong yellow and orange tones and sought out groves of deciduous trees where the fallen leaves carpeted the ground. This autumn scene recalls a series of his paintings entitled Les Alyscamps (Falling Autumn Leaves) *(1888).*

OPPOSITE

Vincent van Gogh, Trees in the Garden of St. Paul's Hospital, *1889. Armand Hammer Foundation.*

PAGES 30–31

Vincent van Gogh, Field with Poppies, *detail.*

29

RIGHT
A view of the asylum garden at Saint-Rémy from the top of the wall enclosure at its western extremity.

High-elevation view of the courtyard. In midsummer the beds are vibrant with flowering annuals, similar to those in van Gogh's painting Courtyard Garden at Arles Hospital *(1888).*

OPPOSITE
Vincent van Gogh, The Asylum Garden at Saint-Rémy, *1889. Oskar Reinhart Collection, Winterthur, Switzerland.*

THE ASYLUM GARDEN

After his release from the hospital, van Gogh could not go outdoors without being taunted by mischievous children who considered him a madman and threw stones at him whenever he set up his easel. He reacted violently to their antics, and the ridicule only increased. His tantrums and seizures worsened, and he learned about the Asylum of Saint-Paul for the treatment of mental patients at Saint-Rémy, a small medieval town on the other side of the nearby Alpilles mountain range. He journeyed there by cart and sequestered himself behind its prisonlike walls. But the asylum offered no cure. Staffed by nuns, it was a depressing place inside, and he continued to have severe mood swings, which are reflected in his paintings. During these times he created sinister images of menacing beetles on funereal white roses, poisonous hooded arums, a death's-head moth, and twisted tree trunks girdled with suffocating ivy. There were periods when he tried to commit suicide by swallowing his oil paints. The director confiscated them, and van Gogh was forbidden to walk beyond the walls without a warden.

During stable periods van Gogh rejoiced at the beauty of the asylum's flowering shrubs, its towering pine trees, and the spectacular countryside beyond its walls. "Considering my life is spent mostly in the garden, it is not so unhappy," he reflected in a letter to Theo. He likened the garden's dark recesses to bowers where lovers might meet. When his paints were returned and he resumed work, an ancient Roman quarry became a favorite motif, its overgrown cliff faces, stone slabs, and ledges depicted as an enormous rock garden. A warden took him to a scenic gorge with a stream cascading through, and he painted it in the style of a Japanese landscape of waterfalls, rock outcrops, tussocks of heath, and weather-beaten pines.

*G*round-level view of the courtyard. Note how the blue and yellow
walls have changed little over the
intervening years since van Gogh's
painting Courtyard Garden
at Arles Hospital (1888).

OPPOSITE

A view of the asylum garden at Saint-Rémy, where van Gogh lived for a year while being treated for mental problems. Since shrub roses have a rugged constitution, which allows them to live more than a hundred years, this may be the same rose he described as "a bush of pale roses in the cold shadow" in a letter to his brother. In this large walled garden, several sycamore trees in the background provide cooling shade while fragrant white mock orange and a yellow kerria shrub help to disguise the wall.

RIGHT

A cathedral of tall trees, including sycamores and chestnuts, arches over a path leading to the director's office at the Asylum of Saint-Paul. The avenue of trees provided comfort for van Gogh and a sense of security after he had been harassed and tormented by street urchins during his painting excursions around Arles.

An olive orchard beside the asylum inspired a series of images showing the trees at various times of the day and depicting different climatic conditions. Van Gogh felt compelled to prove that olive trees in a painting by Gauguin (*Christ in the Garden of Olives,* 1889) looked anemic. The gnarled trunks and contorted branches in his own work seem to writhe with energy against dramatic skies and nurturing soil. He wrote to Theo: "If you could see the olive groves just now! The leaves like old silver, and silver turning to green against the blue, and the orange-colored plowed earth. It is something quite different from your idea of it in the North. It is like the pollarded willows of our Dutch meadows or the oak bushes of our dunes; the rustle of an olive grove has something very secret in it, and immensely old."

Gauguin's painting festered in his mind, as did a similar rendition by Gauguin's artist friend Emile Bernard. He felt that Bernard especially failed to get the least idea of its potential and reality. When van

Gogh completed his own olive orchard studies, he told Theo: "I have worked this month in the olive groves because Bernard and Gauguin have maddened me with their 'Christs in the Garden,' with nothing really observed. . . . I have written that I considered that to think, not dream, was their duty, so that I was aston-

Van Gogh admired bearded irises grown in the asylum garden. One of his most cherished paintings, Irises (1889), shows a strong blue and orange complementary color harmony, the orange from a background of calendulas and the clay soil. A similar color harmony using blue irises can be made with the Siberian wallflower variety 'Orange Bedder'.

ished to see from their work how they had let themselves go. It is not that it leaves me cold, but it gives me a painful feeling of collapse instead of progress."

Local gardens beyond the walls of the asylum were filled with irises and calendulas, and he captured their brilliance as no other artist had before him. Indeed, he painted more than one hundred canvases during his year's stay at Saint-Rémy—almost all of them within sight of the asylum and at least twenty-eight within the garden of the asylum itself.

OPPOSITE
The Asylum of Saint-Paul is located in the shadow of the Alpilles Mountains, part of the Maritime Alps. Van Gogh journeyed into the mountains searching for motifs and discovered a rocky ravine like this with a stream and waterfalls. In spring the roads that twist and wind through the Maritime Alps provide spectacular views bright with such wildflowers as red poppy and yellow Spanish broom, seen here.

Van Gogh often portrayed the sun rising above fields of wheat and casting its life-giving energy over the land. Here a warming early-morning sun penetrates a screen of leafy trees to cast its light over a garden of ornamental grasses, which stand in for van Gogh's wheat fields.

RIGHT

A beautiful billowing cloud of tufted hair grass is the perfect foil for the spiky, rigid flower stems of purple vervain, red orache, and white yarrow in a Dutch garden. Note also the shimmering white flowers of annual fleabane in the background, which add a glittering quality. This type of plant partnership, involving the soft flowing lines of grasses and the sparkle of wayside flowers, was an effect van Gogh sought in nature.

GRASSES AND WHEAT FIELDS

While institutionalized, van Gogh read a great deal and particularly admired a poem written by Walt Whitman about the beauty in a blade of grass. He had started painting grasses in Paris, notably wheat fields, their swaying leaf blades expressing movement and energy. At Saint-Rémy he painted close-ups of wild sedges and oat grasses spangled with wildflowers, sometimes with the fissured bark of a pine tree trunk to provide textural contrast and a sense of scale.

From his bedroom window in the asylum, van Gogh had a clear view of a hay field enclosed by a stout stone wall. He painted the scene several times from his elevated perspective, the stone wall taking on the quality of a picture frame to display a rich play of colors from the meadow grasses.

Perhaps nothing revealed his special fondness for grasses and wheat fields more than his response to a letter from his sister in which she compared the prospect of her losing a sick friend to a plant deprived of rainfall.

"Well, what shall I say about your little literary sketch about plants and rain?" he began his reply.

You see yourself that in nature many flowers are crushed underfoot, get frozen or scorched by the sun, and further that not every grain of wheat, after ripening, returns to the earth, there to germinate and become a new plant—but that the great majority of grains of wheat do not attain their natural development but go to the mill, isn't that true?

Now, as for comparing mankind to grains of corn, in every man who is healthy and natural there is a germinating force as in a grain of wheat. And so natural life is germination. What the germination force is in a grain of wheat, love is in us.

Now, I think we are apt to stand staring with a long face, and at a loss of words, as soon as we are frustrated in our natural development, and see this germination made impossible, and find ourselves placed in a situation as hopeless as that of wheat between the millstones must be.

The metaphor of the wheat is visually presented in van Gogh's painting *The Sower* (1888), in which three-quarters of the canvas shows a newly plowed field in amazing colors. Although the general impression is

forcefully presented that it is hard to conceive of any image that could convey a greater respect for such a humble product as soil. Clearly, in van Gogh's perception, good soil is the foundation of strong growth.

DR. GACHET'S GARDEN

Van Gogh seemed content to stay at the asylum indefinitely, until he received news that Theo planned to marry. Soon after the wedding Theo's wife, Johanna, was pregnant. If the child was a boy, she wrote to her brother-in-law, they would name him after his uncle. After the boy's birth, van Gogh yearned to be near his godchild and discharged himself from the asylum over the objection of its director. As a precaution against further recurrences of his mental problems, he placed himself in the charge of Dr. Paul Gachet, a doctor of psychology, who had previously treated Cézanne, Pissarro, and Renoir for melancholy. Van Gogh admired the doctor's collection of Impressionist art and befriended him.

Dr. Gachet lived at Auvers-sur-Oise, just north of Paris, and there van Gogh was pleased to discover a village largely untouched by the influence of the great city. Along narrow roads edging the River Oise, the village's comfortable thatched cottages seemed to grow out of the surrounding countryside, with colorful pocket-handkerchief gardens, stout stone walls, stone steps, and stone wellheads adding decorative accents that complemented the verdure and steeply sloping land. The residents were mostly farmers, and immense fields were planted with wheat.

Van Gogh rented a room above a café within walking distance of the doctor's house and was often invited to dine with the eccentric widowed doctor. Soon he was enamored of the doctor's nineteen-year-old daughter, Marguerite. He painted her romantically in a pink dress seated at the piano and also in the doctor's garden dressed in white, looking like a

that the soil is violet, it is actually a mosaic, including yellow and white, blue and pink. The picture is a seemingly simple composition, yet it is a parable of life, the sower's seed cast onto the plowed field but also onto a swale where it will never reach its full development. Across the top of the plowed field a band of ripe wheat glows burnished orange beneath a rising sun that is an intense yellow, casting its life-giving warmth and light over the field to make the seeds germinate and grow.

Van Gogh gave the soil a majesty never seen before in artistic expression and never likely to be seen again. The nurturing power of the earth (as well as the energy of the sun to stimulate growth) is so bride in a wedding garden among the pale flowers she grew mostly for cutting. He named the plants—"aloes, cypresses, marigolds, white roses, some vines and a figure, and a cluster of ranunculuses besides." In the village he discovered a beautiful flower garden planted by the widow of landscape artist Charles Daubigny, and an island bed on the front lawn became the focus of a painting he called "one of my most purposeful canvases."

The wheat fields on a plateau above the village were awesome—extending beyond the horizon and laid out like a patchwork quilt. The fields followed the contours of the land, occasionally intersected by wheel tracks. Van Gogh painted the fields in different stages of ripening—lime green and silver in spring; later yellow, then beige; and finally the color of burnished gold. The result was some of the most powerful images of his career, but his paintings still failed to sell and were heaped with ridicule. Monet expressed admiration for his art but did not make a purchase; Dr. Gachet also liked van Gogh's art, but acquired his paintings only as payment for services. During his lifetime van Gogh sold only one canvas—*The Red Vineyard* (1887), painted at Arles.

Troubled by recurring bouts of epilepsy, distraught over the illness of Theo's son, which put a severe emotional and financial strain on Theo's resources, and perhaps feeling Dr. Gachet's disapproval of his friendship with Marguerite, van Gogh slipped into deeper depression. Saying he wanted to scare away crows that were bothering him in a wheat field, he borrowed a gun from Dr. Gachet but shot himself in the stomach in a suicide attempt. Though he was able to stumble into the village for help, the bullet could not be removed and he died two days later, at the age of thirty-seven. He was buried in a tiny churchyard on a windswept hillside overlooking the village of Auvers, among the wheat fields. The grave is still there,

its simple stone slab bearing his name. Vast wheat fields still surround the stone walls of the cemetery, and it is hard to imagine a more appropriate resting place for a person so in harmony with nature. Crows and skylarks abound, and poppies and other wayside flowers still grow along the verges of the road leading up from the village. Visitors from all over the world walk to the site daily in a steady stream, entire families often bringing with them stalks of wheat, bunches of wildflowers, and stems of homegrown sunflowers to lay on the austere ivy-covered gravesite. In the adjacent plot rests his brother, who died six months later, his heart filled with grief.

Van Gogh's artistic career spanned only ten years and yet he produced a staggering amount of work, including some of the most important and beloved paintings ever created. "I want to do images that *touch* some people," he wrote to Theo. "I wish to express not sentimental melancholy, but serious sorrow. . . . I want to progress so far that people will say of my work, he feels deeply, he feels tenderly—not withstanding my so-called roughness, perhaps even because of it. What am I in most people's eyes? A nonentity, or an eccentric and disagreeable man—somebody who has no position in society and never will have, in short the lowest of the low. Very well . . . then I should want any work to show what is in the heart of an eccentric, of such a nobody. This is my ambition, which is, in spite of everything, founded less on anger than on love."

Located in a cemetery among the wheat fields, van Gogh's grave site is almost always decorated with stems of flowers or wheat picked from the roadside or garden-grown.

color HARMONIES

"Cornflowers and white chrysanthemums and a certain number of marigolds—a motif in blue and orange. . . . Heliotrope and yellow roses—a motif in lilac and yellow. . . . Poppies and red geraniums in vigorous green leaves. . . . These are fundamentals that one may subdivide further, and elaborate, but quite enough to show you without the help of a picture that there are colors which cause each other to shine brilliantly, which form a couple, which complete each other like man and woman."

LETTER TO HIS SISTER WILHELMIEN (1888)

A *simple partnership of blue and yellow using yellow miniature daffodils and blue forget-me-nots.*

Vincent van Gogh,
Undergrowth with
Two Figures, *detail*
of undergrowth.

I

T IS NOW MORE THAN ONE HUNDRED years since Vincent van Gogh ended his life, and considering the circumstances of his death, his art could easily have died with him. That it did not is all the more remarkable because Theo soon followed his brother to the grave, tormented by a delirium symptomatic of his brother's mental condition. Sadly, Vincent's younger sister Wil also fell victim to mental illness, ending her days in a mental institution. The widowed Johanna, with no means of support in Paris, returned to her native Holland with her child, Vincent, and struggled to establish an income running a boardinghouse.

There has been much speculation about why van Gogh killed himself. No doubt the suicide was in large part the act of a man in the grip of mental illness, one disillusioned and disappointed by his failure as an artist. But his motive undoubtedly includes other elements. We know from his letters that he considered himself a financial burden on his brother. Theo's limited resources were stretched further with the birth of his son, whose fragile health demanded significant medical attention. Van Gogh's concern for the child—and his suspicion that Theo's support for his painting career deprived the boy of needed care—may have preyed on his deeply depressed mind and contributed to his decision to end his life. In any event, his death from a self-inflicted gunshot wound was devastating to Theo and his family.

Following the death of Theo, his widow, Johanna, inherited her brother-in-law's vast quantity of sketches, letters, and paintings. In her spare time over the years, she promoted, cataloged, and exhibited his work, and through her tenacity and diligence, they began to earn recognition as great works of art. When she passed away in 1927, her son, Vincent (van Gogh's godson), took up the cause of promoting international acclaim for his uncle's art. Now, long

peach orchards of Montmajour. To see them in real life is crucial in order to understand van Gogh's appreciation of particular landscapes and gardens.

When we analyze van Gogh's art, the dominant appeal is his application of *color,* particularly its vibrancy and vitality. When we view his work, we can sense the physical world with intensity—the warmth of the sun, the cold of a snowscape, the chill of a wind-whipped sea, the blustery blasts of the mistral wind, the perfumed gaiety of a sun-drenched cutting garden, the quiet eeriness of a woodland garden, the soft wonder of a night sky. Commenting on a canvas of his olive trees, van Gogh wrote that it would "give the sense of the country and smell of the soil."

The vibrancy of his art comes not only from the tonal values he chose but, more important, from the *color combinations* he created. Often these are pairs like orange and violet, even black and white, but often they are triad harmonies like blue, pink, and white or yellow, black, and orange. In a letter to Theo in the summer of 1888, he explained the intensity of his studies of color: "I am always in hope of making a discovery there, to express the love of two lovers by a wedding of two complementary colors, their mingling *and* their opposition, the mysterious vibrations of kindred tones."

Discussing his reasons for moving to the South of France, he wrote emphatically to an artist friend: "From Arles onwards you are bound to find beautiful contrasts of red and green, of blue and orange, of sulphur and lilac." These are the same color combinations he told Wilhelmien to try in her garden, using flowers to paint the landscape.

Whenever he saw a particularly beautiful color combination in the Provençal landscape, he dashed off a detailed description to Theo. As he explored Arles, he reported: "Everywhere and all over the vault of heaven is a marvelous blue, and the sun sheds a radiance of pure sulphur, and it is soft and as lovely as

LEFT
The combination of orange and violet blue can be achieved by contrasting petal colors with surrounding hardscape elements, such as walls. These orange gerbera daisies create one of van Gogh's favorite color harmonies as they stand against a blue courtyard wall, perfectly illustrating how his sometimes grand landscapes can be interpreted in a small space.

after van Gogh's technique has ceased to be ridiculed, exhibitions of his work—and payment for his paintings at auction—continue to set world records.

Amazingly, a large number of the gardens and landscapes that van Gogh depicted survive to the present day, and it is possible to visit the sites: the colorful courtyard garden he painted in the Arles hospital; the Garden of the Poets in Arles; the sinister asylum garden at Saint-Rémy; Dr. Gachet's garden, where he painted the doctor's daughter; Daubigny's garden, with its colorful island beds; the sparkling wildflower meadows, lavender fields, and olive orchards of Provence; the vast wheat fields of Auvers; the writhing black junipers against the rocky limestone slopes of the Alpilles Mountains; the quaint thatched cottages and gardens of Saintes-Maries-de-la-Mer; the sparkling apple, plum, and

Vincent van Gogh,
Field with Poppies, 1889.
Kunsthalle, Bremen.

An example of a monochromatic color planting using shades of red, including daylilies, Maltese cross, and 'Meidiland Red' shrub roses.

the combination of heavenly blue and yellows as a van der Meer of Delft. I cannot paint it as beautiful as that, but it absorbs me so much that I let myself go, never thinking of a single rule."

THE COLOR WHEEL

Though van Gogh ignored rules, seeking his best color combinations in nature, and especially in the gardens he visited, he was well aware of the scientific basis of color relationships. The first color wheel had been published in 1839, showing the scientific relationship between colors. Before then, the British physicist Sir Isaac Newton had identified the colors of sunlight by shining light through a glass prism. The prism split the sun's rays into the six main colors evident whenever we see a rainbow—red, yellow, orange, green, blue, and violet.

However, it was not until Michel-Eugène Chevreul, a chemist working for the Gobelins dye works in Paris, published the first chromatic wheel that van Gogh could clearly understand the laws of colors and see how all colors are linked and derived from the three primaries—red, yellow, and blue. The other colors of the rainbow—green, orange, and violet—are produced by an overlapping or mixing of the primaries—yellow and red to produce orange; blue and yellow to produce green; and blue and red to produce violet. Chevreul divided his wheel into "hot colors" (those that are assertive, like orange, red, and yellow) and "cool colors" (those that tend to recede, like blue, green, and purple). He explained that colors opposite each other on the wheel (for example, yellow and violet) make the best contrasts, and that placing two separate colors close to each other or entwined (as in the threads of a fabric) produces the same effect as mixing the colors. Van Gogh was so captivated with Chevreul's concept of entwining that he kept balls of complementary colored wool in a lacquered box.

CONCEPTS OF COLOR HARMONIES AND CONTRASTS

"Spring is tender young shoots of wheat and pink apple blossoms. Autumn is the contrast of yellow leaves with shades of violet. Winter is white with black silhouettes. If summer is taken to be a contrast of blues with the orange of golden, bronze grain, it is possible to paint a picture in complementary colors for every one of the seasons." LETTER TO THEO (SUMMER 1889)

COMPLEMENTARY COLOR CONTRASTS involve pairing opposites on the color wheel, a technique evident in van Gogh's work. His favorites were the contrast of red and green, yellow and violet, and blue and orange. When pairing opposites, avoid using the colors in equal strengths or the effect will seem monotonous. Stippling with white will enliven these color contrasts.

MONOCHROMATIC HARMONIES consist of pure colors (red, blue, or yellow, for example) in association with tints and tones of the pure colors (such as red, pale pink, rosy pink, and deep pink). The best combinations involving monochromatic harmonies allow one color to dominate (for example a crimson red). White can be added sparingly to brighten a monochromatic presentation.

ANALOGOUS COLOR HARMONIES are colors adjacent to each other on the color wheel, such as green, blue, and violet (a cool color combination) or red, orange, and yellow (a hot combination). White can be used to intensify a hot color harmony and enliven a cool one; black can tone down a hot color harmony and further temper a cool one.

TRIADIC COLOR HARMONIES use three colors that are usually equidistant on the color wheel, such as yellow, orange, and blue. Van Gogh's most appealing triadic color combination is the red, green, and silver in his painting *The Poppy Fields* (1888), silver coming from the gray-green foliage of lavender. Since silver is not evident on the color wheel, this triad can be appreciated only by studying nature. The triadic grouping of red, yellow, and orange produces a hot color harmony; blue, violet, and mauve a cool harmony. Since white is the color of intense heat (we often say something is "white hot"), it can be used to intensify a hot color triad; and since white is the color we associate with snow and ice, it can be used effectively to make cool color harmonies sparkle.

POLYCHROMATIC COLOR HARMONIES use a multitude of colors. The most pleasing polychromatic combination is a rainbow. In the garden a beautiful polychromatic harmony can be achieved by grouping together the entire color spectrum of a particular flower (all pansies, all primroses, or all irises). Van Gogh's friend Gauguin liked polychromatic harmonies and would introduce a discordant color deliberately to startle his audience—such as a splash of yellow among pinks, blues, and violets. Van Gogh was briefly influenced by Gauguin during their sojourn together in Arles, and van Gogh's painting from that period, *Memory of the Garden at Etten* (1888), in which he painted from memory rather than directly from nature, is the best example of his use of a polychromatic color harmony. His painting *Courtyard Garden at Arles Hospital* (1888) is also an excellent example of a polychromatic harmony, with each of its pie-shaped beds containing a vibrant mixture of annuals.

In his writings Chevreul even suggested ways of applying his laws of colors to the garden, and subsequently two French garden writers—J. Decaisne and C. Naudin—elaborated on Chevreul's thesis in their book *Manuel de l'amateur de jardin*. In particular, they explained the important role of white in a landscape, especially its ability to enliven any color it is placed next to. White has the added benefit, they remarked, of improving poor combinations of colors, such as red and blue or purple and violet.

Van Gogh endorsed this concept in a letter to an artist friend from Arles. "Take *The Sower*," he wrote. "The picture is divided in half; one half, the upper part, is yellow; the lower part is violet. Well, the white trousers allow the eye to rest and distract it at the moment when the excessive simultaneous contrast of yellow and violet would irritate it."

It was not only familiarity with Chevreul's laws of colors that sharpened van Gogh's response to color but also his own astute observations of the natural or cultivated landscape—especially from viewing gardens and through painting still life arrangements using both cultivated and wayside plants. These revealed to him the best color harmonies and color contrasts. Sometimes the color combinations he discovered on his walks had a dramatic impact on his sensitivity. The red and green combination, for example, reminded him of "the terrible passions of humanity."

Van Gogh identified pairs of colors with particular seasons of the year: yellow and green represented spring, orange and violet were summery, red and orange meant autumn, and black and white emulated the starkness of winter. Black and white was perhaps the most intriguing color harmony of all. In his mind black could be maroon—like the flowers of "black" scabiosa—or it could be dark brown, bottle green, or deep purple; moreover, white could be silvery white, like the dried seed cases of the money plant, or a green-

Van Gogh had a lacquered box filled with balls of colored wool in colors he often used in his paintings. Some of the balls were composed of two threads entwined, aiding his ability to recognize the most beautiful color partnerships.

ish white, like the hooded spathes of arums. Whenever van Gogh found an interesting new color grouping during his walks, he would write about it enthusiastically.

His quest to find stimulating color groupings was never expressed more dramatically than in a letter to Wilhelmien: "The more ugly, old, vicious, ill, poor I get, the more I want to take my revenge by producing a brilliant color, well arranged, resplendent. Jewelers, too, get old and ugly before they learn how to arrange precious stones well. And arranging the colors in a picture in order to make them vibrate and to enhance their value by contrasts is something like arranging jewels properly—or designing costumes."

Or planting a garden, he might have added, for in another letter he declared: "Sometimes by erring one finds the right road. Go make up for it by painting your garden just as it is."

Significantly, it was the great British plantswoman Gertrude Jekyll who took the fundamentals of van Gogh's color theories (and those of other painters of the Impressionist era) and used them for even more elaborate effects. A painter herself before failing eyesight caused her to stop, she experimented at her home, Munstead Wood, with color harmonies she discovered in Impressionist paintings. She recognized that separate color theme areas could also be connected for subtle sensuous effects, such as a cool color garden adjacent to a predominantly yellow and orange garden. "To pass from the cool quiet colourings of lavender and pink into the golden garden is like stepping into sunshine," she wrote.

Following are the most familiar color combinations seen in van Gogh's paintings and referred to in his letters, beginning with the most popular.

YELLOW AND BLUE

Although orange and blue are opposites on the color wheel and make the most powerful contrast when placed together, yellow and blue offer a similarly pleasing contrast, and in van Gogh's letters it is the contrast of blue and yellow that he referred to repeatedly when describing paintings and gardens. Writing to a young artist friend, Emile Bernard, shortly after his move to Arles, he observed: "The town is surrounded by immense meadows all in bloom with countless buttercups—a sea of yellow— in the foreground these meadows are divided by a ditch full of blue irises."

In a letter to Theo written in the summer of 1888, he eagerly anticipated autumn because "when the leaves start to fall . . . when all the foliage is yellow, it will be amazing against the blue."

Van Gogh's most famous yellow and blue partnership is found in his painting of violet blue irises against a citron yellow background, *Vase with Irises Against a Yellow Background* (1889). But yellow and blue is a repetitive theme in many other landscape paintings, notably *View of Arles with Irises in the Foreground* (1889), *Daubigny's Garden* (1890), and *Undergrowth with Two Figures* (1890).

Whenever I plant yellow flowers, I try to partner them with blue, and vice versa. Some particularly striking plant partnerships include yellow daffodils surrounded by blue forget-me-nots; blue salvias against a background of yellow perennial foxgloves; and blue veronicas in company with yellow rudbeckia daisies. My personal favorite blue and yellow partnership is fragrant yellow azalea 'Mollis' underplanted with Spanish or English bluebells.

YELLOW, BLUE, AND ORANGE. Van Gogh extended the coupling of yellow and blue to include orange as a triadic color combination. Indeed, in a dogmatic letter to Theo shortly after arriving in Arles, he stated: *"There is no blue without yellow and without orange,* and if you put in blue, then you must also put in yellow, and orange, too, mustn't you?"

This stunning example of a monochromatic planting in Brittany is evocative of van Gogh's powerful sunflower paintings. Yellow highlights come not only from yellow flowers (notably daylily 'Golden Chimes' and Marguerite daisies) but also from yellow and green variegated sage.

The contrast of blue and yellow is especially beautiful among irises. In this bog garden yellow flag iris (Iris pseudacorus) and blue Siberian iris (Iris siberica) flower together among spiky leaves.

In this yellow and blue perennial border, the predominant plants are yellow Lysimachia punctata and blue Salvia x superba.

The complementary color combination of yellow and blue is achieved here using spiky flowers against an old stone wall at Château de Canon in Normandy. The yellow is Lysimachia punctata *and the blue is* Veronica spicata.

Within a year of his arrival in Arles, van Gogh's mental state deteriorated and he admitted himself to a nearby institution for the treatment of mental disease, the Asylum of Saint-Paul, at Saint-Rémy. There, within the walls of the asylum, was a beautiful garden with towering mature umbrella pines and groves of redbuds girdled with ivy. The predominantly green garden had a calming effect and he quickly painted several impressions, telling Theo:

Like the flickering brushstrokes of an Impressionist painting, blue, yellow, and orange pansies create one of van Gogh's favorite triadic color harmonies.

> *Here is a new size 30 canvas, once again as commonplace as a chromo in the little shops, which represents the eternal nests of greenery for lovers.*
>
> *Some thick tree trunks covered in ivy, the ground also covered in ivy and periwinkle, a stone bench and a bush of pale roses in the cold shadow. In the foreground some plants with white calyxes. It is green, violet, and pink.*
>
> *Since I have been here, the deserted garden planted with large pines beneath which the grass grows tall and unkempt, and mixed with various weeds, has sufficed for my work. . . . However, the countryside around Saint-Rémy is very beautiful, and I will probably widen my field of endeavor.*

During his stay in Saint-Rémy, on a walk around the walls of the asylum, he found the garden of a farmer's wife, mostly blue irises and yellow and orange calendulas planted in reddish, flinty soil. They are the principal components of his famous blue, yellow, and orange painting, *Irises* (1889).

The color contrast of blue and pink—also blue, pink, and white—came to van Gogh as a revelation as he walked out into the countryside around Arles and saw orchards in bloom, most noticeably with peach trees. He also painted almonds, pears, and plums in a frenzy of creative energy, describing himself as "hard at it, painting with the enthusiasm of a Marseillais eating bouillabaisse." In a letter to Bernard, he observed: "I am working on six pictures of fruit trees in bloom. And what I brought home today would probably please you—it is a dug-up square of earth in an orchard with a fence of rushes and two peach trees in full bloom. Pink against a scintillating blue sky with white clouds, and in the sunshine."

The title of the painting he described is *Peach Tree in Blossom* (1888), which he declared to be the best landscape he had done. With its emphasis on a myriad of flower blossoms, this canvas inspired a planting at my farm that fills one's entire field of vision with pink blossoms against blue skies. I've achieved this by combining several flowering trees in a rosy pink monochromatic color combination, three distinct varieties blooming together to create a dazzling floral display. They are redbuds (*Cercis canadensis*), lavender pink azaleas (*Rhododendron poukhanense*), and several pink crab apples, which open pink but quickly fade to white. Against the sky these extremely floriferous trees perfectly capture the vibrancy of van Gogh's blue, pink, and white motif. Moreover, at one point the path crossing this expanse of pink steeply descends a hill, and the blossoms from the hillside frame an arched rusty red bridge crossing a stream.

Coincidentally, blue and pink is a color combination that Monet also found appealing after a visit to the Mediterranean, and he later used it in his garden at Giverny. There he painted his house pink so that blue flowers would look good against the facade, and

he painted the walls of a separate house blue so that pink flowers would look good against the blue backdrop.

GREEN IN THE GARDEN

Many gardeners fail to see why a color as common as green is worth bothering about, since green is the predominant hue of foliage and grass against which other colors must contrast. But there are many gradations of green, including bright lemony greens and

dark black-greens, both of which are colors van Gogh seized upon to portray dramatic leafy contrasts in his garden paintings.

Also, foliage offers *texture* and *form* to consider, ranging from the smooth, slender leaves of willow, iris, and bamboo to the deeply indented, leathery leaves of fig trees and ivy and the velvety, serrated leaves of poppies.

Van Gogh identified green with intimacy and morality. In a description of a public garden across the street from his lodgings in Arles, he told Theo: "I am in a public garden, quite close to the street of the

OPPOSITE
The allure of pink and blue is never greater than in a naturalistic planting of fragrant hyacinths, flowering beside a pond that resembles one van Gogh painted at his father's parsonage garden in Holland. Although white and red are also included, pink and blue dominate to create a cool springtime effect.

With his painting entitled The Garden of the Poets (1888), van Gogh proved the power of green to decorate a landscape, noting how textures and structural qualities aided in the composition. In this small shady planting, the broad blue-green, paddle-shaped leaves of hostas make an effective contrast with the fleecy light green fronds of maidenhair ferns and the silvery leaves of a Japanese painted fern.

The influence of the Japanese on van Gogh's art is reflected in this informal shaded moss garden. Though the Japanese elements are understated (a small stone lantern and sculpture), the rich tapestry of greens and the strong, sinuous woody elements from vines, trunks, and branches evoke a secret glade he described.

kind girls hardly ever went, although we took a walk in the gardens practically every day. This side of the garden is also, for the same reason of chastity or morality, destitute of any flowering bushes like oleanders. There are ordinary plane trees, pines in stiff clumps, a weeping tree, and the green grass. But it is all so intimate. Manet has gardens like this."

Branches of a sugar maple and the spiky stems of lilies help to frame a tapestry garden inspired by the design philosophy in van Gogh's description of The Garden of the Poets (1888), a public park in Arles.

One of van Gogh's most lyrical descriptions of the same garden is contained in a subsequent letter to Theo. It is, in fact, a perfect description of what garden designers today would call a foliage garden or a tapestry or green garden. He was moved to title his painting *The Garden of the Poets* (1888), as he imagined it to be a perfectly romantic spot for poets to compose their lines. Although in this letter he referred to some pink oleander flowers, it is the green components that dominate. The passage also indicates that he changed the plantings slightly in his painting to satisfy his own aesthetic ideal:

Since seven o'clock this morning I have been sitting in front of something that after all is no great matter, a clipped round bush of cedar or cypress growing amid grass. You already know this clipped bush because you already have a study of the garden. Enclosed also is a sketch of my canvas, again a square size 30.

The bush is green, touched a little with bronze and various other tints. The grass is bright, bright green, malachite touched with citron, and the sky is bright, bright blue. The row of bushes in the background is all oleanders, raving mad; the blasted things are flowering so riotously they may well catch locomotor ataxia. They are loaded with fresh flowers and quantities of faded flowers as well, and their green is continually renewing itself in fresh, strong shoots, apparently inexhaustibly. A funereal cypress is standing over them, and some small figures are sauntering along a pink path.

This makes a pendant to another size 30 canvas of the same spot, only from a totally different angle, in which the whole garden is in quite different greens, under a sky of pale citron.

But isn't it true that this garden has a fantastic character that makes you quite able to imagine the poets of the Renaissance, Dante, Petrarch, Boccaccio, strolling among these bushes and over the flowery grass? It is true that I have left out some trees, but what I have kept in the composition is really there just as you see it. Only it has been overcrowded with some shrubs that are not in character.

And to get at that character, the fundamental truth of it; that's three times now that I've painted the same spot.

For gardeners today, foliage gardens can work especially well in shady areas—not only on a similar scale to van Gogh's relatively large poets' garden but also in small spaces. Many kinds of green are available to gardeners, but it is also worth using variegated foliage, which tends to be either white and green (producing a silvery look from a distance) or yellow and green, which often produces a chartreuse or golden appearance.

The first foliage garden I developed after reading van Gogh's philosophy about the poets' garden was influenced by his admiration for Japanese art and

Vincent van Gogh, The
Garden of the Poets, *1888.*
The Art Institute of Chicago,
Mr. and Mrs. Lewis Larned
Coburn Memorial Collection.

Vincent van Gogh, Les
Alyscamps (Falling Autumn
Leaves), 1888. Kröller-Müller
Museum, Otterlo, Netherlands.

gardens. It incorporates the three essential elements of a Japanese garden—evergreen accents, rocks, and water. The Japanese theme is heightened by a sculptural element in the form of a Japanese maiden and a Japanese lantern on a small stone promontory. In a grove of plum trees with a small ravine, I pruned away all low branches to emphasize the canopy so that in spring the plums produce an umbrella of white blossoms similar to van Gogh's orchard scenes. Several wild fox grapes twine sinuously up into the leaf canopy and produce a deeply shaded site that uses mostly hostas, ferns, and Japanese hakone grass for its green components and textural effects. A stream runs through to provide the music of water so essential to Japanese landscapes. It is skirted by a path of pine needles from evergreen junipers (van Gogh always called them cypresses in his letters, but they are in fact junipers). Ivy has been trained to girdle the trees to emulate the "nests of greenery" in van Gogh's asylum garden, and cushions of moss have been introduced to emphasize the feeling of tranquillity. The path makes a sweep through the foliage accents to a rusty red bridge that crosses the stream to a sunny bog garden.

The sunny bog (or swamp) garden features a big collection of blue Japanese water irises and yellow European flag irises. From there the path enters a "leaf tunnel," which is a grassy path meandering through maple trees that have been pruned of lower branches to create a cathedral effect. This is similar in style to van Gogh's paintings of woodland and undergrowth, such as *Path in the Woods* (1887) and *Undergrowth* (1887), both painted in Paris. On both sides of the green path are woodland wildflowers, such as blue phlox and English primroses, and spring bulbs, such as daffodils and bluebells. Though the leaf tunnel is predominantly green in spring and summer, as in van Gogh's paintings, in autumn it becomes a tunnel of gold, as in his painting of autumn leaves in *Les Alyscamps* (1888), in which towering poplars have dropped their leaves to create a yellow carpet.

The most spectacular foliage garden I've made is true to van Gogh's rendering of *The Garden of the Poets* (1888). On a barren hillside with a lone weeping willow bordering a stream, I added trees and shrubs with contrasting leaves to present a panorama of van Gogh's greens—from yellow-green (from the majestic weeping willow) through silvery green (from perennial maiden grass and Russian olive) to black-green (from a towering Lawson cypress that pierces the sky like a church spire). A weeping forsythia and a weeping cherry—both in middle greens—help to provide extra contrasts of texture and form. At a particular vantage point the branches of a sugar maple frame the tapestry, blocking out all extraneous elements from adjacent areas, including sweeps of lawn and sky, so that the scene looks like a living painting and brings to life precisely the effect that van Gogh so beautifully described and painted.

RED AND GREEN

Van Gogh considered red and green to express passion, and he identified their contrast as one of the strongest he could make using complementary colors. Bubbling with enthusiasm over the progress of his work in the South of France, he wrote to Theo: "Ah, these farm gardens with their lovely big red Provençal roses, and the vines and the fig trees! It is all a poem, and the eternal bright sunshine too, in spite of which the foliage is very green."

The complement of red and green on the color wheel is the easiest of all his favorite color combinations to emulate in the garden, simply by choosing plants with bright red flowers and healthy green leaves, such as roses and geraniums. The partnership of red

and green is especially effective for small-space plantings like window boxes and patios, where red-flowering potted plants can be enhanced by adding some green foliage plants, such as the chartreuse trailing sweet potato vine and dark green trailing periwinkle.

Taking inspiration from van Gogh's repeated urging to use red and green in the garden, it is easy to create incredibly dramatic red and green color contrasts by grouping a collection of mostly red bedding geraniums along stone walls, walks, or flights of stone steps. This container planting scheme is most beautiful when a light shower of rain turns the stone the

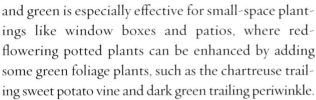

color of charcoal, adding a black element that van Gogh often liked to use in his colorful garden and landscape paintings as a means of softening harsh contrasts.

Another sensational red and green planting scheme involves planting a vigorous shrub rose, such as 'Meidiland Red', in association with red daylilies and red Maltese cross (*Lychnis chalcedonica*). In my own garden a white picket fence helps keep the bushy shrub rose erect, while spires of silvery lamb's ears enliven the motif.

SILVER IN THE GARDEN

With its red and green motif and prominent silver tones, van Gogh's rendering of a poppy field, entitled *Field with Poppies* (1889), found adjacent to the walls of the Asylum of Saint-Paul, is similar in its color values to Monet's painting of a poppy field outside the walls of his garden at Giverny. Art historians have suggested that van Gogh may even have been inspired by Monet's painting, but this is unlikely because he was always quick to acknowledge any inspiration from other artists, especially Monet, whom he revered. Monet had been so impressed by the silvery accents in the meadow he painted (which came from drifts of wild sage) that he transferred the red, green, and silver motif to island beds in his garden, using geraniums for the red and green highlights and an evergreen silver-leaf dianthus for the silver accents; he surrounded the beds with a border of the dianthus.

Van Gogh's liking for silver in a landscape is most forcefully expressed in a letter to Theo toward the end of his stay at the asylum: "Oh, my dear Theo, if you saw the olives just now. . . . The leaves, old silver and silver turning to green against the blue. And the orange-colored plowed earth. It is something quite different from your idea of it in the North, the tender beauty, the distinction."

Unfortunately, the Mediterranean olive tree is too tender for most gardens, as it needs a nearly frost-free climate, but in nature there are many hardy silvery trees (sometimes referred to as gray foliaged) that can substitute for it, including the Russian olive (*Elaeagnus angustifolia*) and the weeping pear (*Pyrus salicifolia* 'Pendula'). Among perennials there is an even wider choice of plants to use for silvery accents, the most common of which is lamb's ears (*Stachys olympica*).

Silver does not have the hotness of white. Indeed, it has a soothing misty quality that is difficult to achieve using white. A big danger of clumping too much white in the garden is its tendency to punch

holes in the landscape, and so white is usually best applied in small dabs, like a sprinkling of salt, using only airy white flowers such as dame's rocket and feverfew. Though van Gogh expressed his pleasure at seeing the contrasts of black and white in a landscape, it is often worth considering whether silver might make a better contrast for the black or if silver in combination with white might produce a lovely softening effect. An all-silver garden would also be beautiful, using foliage effects to make the silver and introducing white flowers sparingly. Like green in the garden, silver seems to go with anything, whereas white might be too garish and distracting.

YELLOW AND ORANGE

Many people recoil from yellow or orange in the garden because they are such assertive colors. Sometimes partnered with red to create a "hot" color harmony, yellow and orange are most often associated with the sun. Indeed, patches of yellow and orange can reflect

the light of a naked sun so brightly the effect is dazzling—completely overpowering other colors with their strength and brilliance.

However, van Gogh so admired the impact of yellow and orange that he painted an entire series of fruits (quinces and lemons) and sunflowers in predominantly yellow and orange tones interrupted only by black highlights as respite from the glare.

In the floral kingdom there are more yellow and orange flowers than any other color (with the possible exception of white), and so it is quite easy to create a "golden" garden that would have pleased van Gogh immeasurably. First, it's important to realize that yellow flowers can vary in hue from a pale, creamy yellow to deep orange, sometimes with yellow "button" centers and other times with black or green. Yellow is not only present in petals; it is often the color of foliage—notably 'Bowles Golden' grass (*Carex elata* 'Aurea') and gold-lace evergreen cypresses. In gardens that strive for a golden theme, it's good to include yellow and creamy foliage to avoid monotony.

When van Gogh began formulating his idea for the sunflowers series, he confided to Theo: "I am thinking of decorating my studio with half a dozen pictures of 'Sunflowers,' a decoration in which the raw or broken chrome yellows will blaze forth on various backgrounds—blue, from the palest malachite green to *royal blue,* framed in thin strips of wood."

Though several of his sunflower paintings have blue backgrounds to effect the blue and yellow color contrast he liked so much, he decided that his favorite painting was one in which the sunflowers, the vase, and the background are all tones of yellow and orange, with just dabs of black to represent the seed discs. He described the effect as "light on light."

I was inspired by van Gogh's concept of "light on light" to plant an all yellow and orange garden using mostly sunflowers, marigolds, and rudbeckias. As in his sunflower paintings, I ensured touches of black by using sunflowers with black seed discs and black-eyed Susans. Simultaneously, I wrote to a dear friend, Olive Dunn—a well-respected New Zealand garden writer—telling her my plan. She enthusiastically took up the challenge herself and produced a "Van Gogh Garden" featuring more of an orange emphasis, using chrysanthemums, marigolds, nasturtiums, Turk's cap lilies, and heleniums. Although some of the orange flowers had black petal markings, additional touches of black were introduced by black violas and bronze foliage.

BLACK IN THE GARDEN

A story is told about Monet's death—that when his funeral hearse was being driven through the streets of Giverny to the graveyard, a black shroud was draped over his coffin. This image of black—with the mourners dressed similarly in black—was too much for Monet's close friend Georges Clemenceau, former prime minister of France. It is said that he suddenly

seized the shroud and stripped it away, declaring, "Black was not part of Monet's palette."

Nevertheless, Monet's greatest masterpiece after his immense waterlily panels is considered to be an early work, *The Magpie* (1869), showing a black and white bird on a wattle fence in a garden covered with snow. Possibly the best example of a black and white motif ever painted, it stunned the art world with its powerful contrasts and today occupies a place of honor in the Musée d'Orsay, in Paris.

Though Monet did tend to exclude a true black from his later paintings, preferring to paint shadows in blue or violet, he knew the value of bold contrasts and continued to use black as a stipple effect. Van Gogh, on the other hand, was almost fanatical about the use of black, not just for shadows and not only as a true black, but also to outline important elements of his compositions—a technique the Impressionists never used. He went to great lengths to explain why he liked black in association with white and also black coupled with orange and yellow. Even the mere suggestion of black—such as maroon or dark green—invariably would be rendered as jet black in van Gogh's paintings.

In nature few flowers are completely black, which is understandable when you consider that flowers must stand out in order to attract pollinators. However, there are numerous flowers with prominent black petal markings. Some common examples include the black and white African daisy known as star of the Veldt (*Venidium fastuosum*), especially the variety 'Zulu'. This flower has not only a black button center but also a black zone at the base of the petals that creates a black ring. There is an orange version that carries the same black pattern. Other black and white flowers include the Oriental poppy 'Perry's White' and the tree peony 'Joseph Rock', both of which have prominent black markings at the base of the petals.

In spite of a scarcity of all-black flowers, there are black violas, hollyhocks, and scabiosas. Some flowers with maroon markings can look black on cloudy days, including maroon peonies, tulips, and nasturtiums.

BLACK AND WHITE

"A technical question. Just give me your opinion on it in your next letter. I am going to put the black and the white boldly on my palette just as the color merchant sells them to us and use them just as they are."
LETTER TO EMILE BERNARD (SPRING 1888)

This letter communicates van Gogh's gleefulness at the prospect of experimenting with such powerful contrasts as black and white. Though his several references to black and white as extreme contrasts relate to their use in landscapes, he did use them in a painting of the asylum entitled *Lilacs* (1889), showing a clump of black iris in company with what appear to be light sprays of white feverfew.

In a letter to Theo he positively bubbled with enthusiasm at the prospect of painting black and white contrasts:

> *Or let us take a more amusing motif: imagine a woman in a black-and-white-checkered dress in the same primitive landscape, with a blue sky and an orange soil—that would be a rather funny sight, I think. In Arles they often do wear black and white checks.*
>
> *Suffice it to say that black and white are also colors, for in many cases they can be looked upon as colors, for their simultaneous contrast is as striking as that of green and red.*

Yet when black and white might make a realistic appearance—to represent the darkness of night and the brightness of illumination, for example—he used neither, notably in his painting *Night Café* (1888), in which the night is expressed in violet tones and gaslight is orange. Even the stars twinkle yellow and blue.

In my garden a number of outbuildings are shaded by tall sugar maple trees for parts of the day. So we

The idea of using black and
orange in a garden was described
in a letter van Gogh wrote about
his painting of a cutting garden
near Arles, entitled Flowering
Garden with Path (1888).
Here the orange elements come
from orange cosmos and tall
orange sunflowers planted
in broad brushstrokes. Black
highlights are introduced by
the seed-bearing discs at the
center of each sunflower head.

have painted the walls and picket fences mostly white, the better to reflect light and produce improved flowering for sun-loving annuals. These white expanses have proven excellent places to plant black elements—especially black hollyhocks (which really are black, though there is also a maroon variety that some seed catalogs call black).

In other areas where we have foliage backgrounds, we often plant both black and white hollyhocks together. However, the most satisfying use of black and white involves black pansies. One variety, 'Jet Black', is as black as coal, and a smaller flowered viola called 'Molly Sanderson' has the same intensely black petals. Van Gogh loved pansies and violas, and so most years we plant a pansy garden in his honor, with the full range of pansy colors, including blue, yellow, and red. But what gives the planting distinction is a drift of black pansies among white feverfew, the two together adding a glittering quality.

Incidentally, pansies can be purchased with either clear colors or black blotches. The whites with black blotches present an instantaneous black and white color contrast, best seen in a small space, such as a window box or urn.

BLACK AND ORANGE

Black scabiosa flowers feature prominently in van Gogh's colorful painting of a cutting garden in Provence, though he contrasted them appealingly with orange and yellow marigolds. Following the completion of this painting, entitled *Flower Garden* (1888), he was inspired to write to Wilhelmien, explaining in detail some of his color theories. He even named the plants depicted in the painting. Bear in mind that "blue blowballs" probably refers to *Nigella damascena* (love-in-a-mist) and Africans is his name for tall marigolds (*Tagetes erecta*):

I have a study of a garden one meter wide, poppies and other red flowers surrounded by green in the foreground, and a square of blue blowballs. Then a bed of orange and yellow Africans, then white and yellow flowers, and at last, in the background, pink and lilac, and also dark violet scabiosas, red geraniums, and sunflowers, and a fig tree and an oleander and a vine. And in the far distance black cypresses against low white houses with orange roofs—and a delicate blue-green streak of sky.

Oh, I know very well that not a single flower is drawn completely, that they are mere dabs of color, red, yellow, orange, green, blue, violet, but the impression of all these colors in their juxtaposition is there all right, in the painting as in nature.

In another letter to Wilhelmien, van Gogh elaborated in more detail about his choice of color harmonies, using specific examples of plants to encourage her to incorporate the plantings in her own garden. He then conjectured: "Explaining the whole theory to you would involve quite a lot of writing, yet it might be done. Colorings, wallpapers, and whatnot could be made much prettier by paying attention to the laws of colors."

By "the laws of colors," it's not clear whether van Gogh was thinking of nature's laws or scientific color theory, since he said in another letter on the subject of color harmonies: ". . . we are still far from the time when people will understand the curious relationship between one fragment of nature and another, which all the same explain each other and enhance each other."

WHITE IN THE GARDEN

One of van Gogh's most evocative garden paintings shows Marguerite, the nineteen-year-old daughter of Dr. Paul Gachet. Dressed in white like a bride, she is surrounded by mostly white, pale pink, and pale yellow flowers, as though standing in what we would

White alone can look too sterile in a garden, but partnered with silver and gray, it comes alive. Note how dark (almost black) vertical accents from spiky seed heads also help to enliven this white garden at the home of Dutch artist Ton ter Linden.

LEFT
Vincent van Gogh,
Daubigny's Garden, *detail.*

OPPOSITE

Vincent van Gogh, Mlle.
Gachet in Her Garden
at Auvers-sur-Oise,
1890. Musée d'Orsay, Paris.

today call a wedding garden. It is thought that van Gogh harbored amorous feelings for Marguerite but was thwarted by the doctor's disapproval. In the painting, entitled *Mlle. Gachet in Her Garden at Auvers-sur-Oise* (1890), the bright garden is seen on top of a sunny hilltop above the Gachet home. She is dressed elegantly in a long white gown and surrounded by mostly white roses or pale yellow marigolds, which match her hat, and she has a hand cupped tenderly around a spray of white roses. The sky is white and pale blue, and the entire scene has a lightness and gaiety about it that is summery and romantic.

Van Gogh rendered another evocative portrait of Marguerite—seated at a piano in a pink dress, again with a romantic use of color, complexion, and line. Marguerite herself confirmed that van Gogh did the portrait while her father was away in Paris and, when the doctor returned to see that his patient had painted her, he was upset at the affection the painting seemed to suggest. In spite of his parental concerns, the doctor allowed van Gogh to paint his daughter again.

White is a romantic color, a popular color for weddings, a symbol of purity. It is a hot color, and its contrast with green is powerful. Green foliage can create dark shadows close to black, and the contrast, while dramatic, is not as stiff or formal as a true black. And white gardens are fun to plant when there is a wealth of white flowers and variegated foliage with white accents.

White is also a good color for twilight or evening gardens. Van Gogh loved the night and once declared that he saw more colors in a night sky than in the daytime. Many flowers are actually night-blooming, and powerfully fragrant to attract night-flying moths and bats, so by carefully choosing varieties, it's possible to create a luminous garden of white flowers that is also highly fragrant.

favorite STRUCTURES

"*I am also thinking of planting two oleanders in tubs by the door.*"

LETTER TO THEO EXPLAINING HOW
HE PROPOSED TO DECORATE THE ENTRANCE
TO HIS NEW LODGINGS (SPRING 1888)

A *wooden cart, used to display daffodils in terra-cotta pots, is similar to several carts van Gogh painted in the countryside around Arles.*

WHEN VAN GOGH reluctantly admitted himself for treatment at the Asylum of Saint-Paul, at Saint-Rémy, he soon cast his eye about for subjects to paint and found the parklike garden alluring in various ways. In addition to many mature trees and groves of lilacs, it was filled with ornamental structural elements, such as benches and a fountain. "Here is the description of a canvas that is in front of me at the moment," he wrote to Theo in the autumn of 1889:

> A view of the park of the asylum where I am staying: on the right a gray terrace and a side wall of the house, some deflowered rosebushes; on the left a stretch of the park— red ocher—the soil scorched by the sun, covered with fallen pine needles. This edge of the park is planted with large pines, whose trunks and branches are red ocher, the foliage green gloomed over by an admixture of black.
>
> These high trees stand out against an evening sky with violet stripes on a yellow ground, which higher turns into pink, into green. A wall—also red ocher—shuts off the view and is topped only by a violet and yellow ocher hill. Now the nearest tree is an enormous trunk, struck by lightning and sawed off. But one side branch shoots up high and lets fall an avalanche of dark green pine needles. The somber giant—like a defeated proud man—contrasts when considered in the nature of a living creature, with the pale smile of a last rose on the fading bush in front of him. Underneath the trees, empty stone benches, sullen box trees; the sky is mirrored yellow in a puddle left by the rain. A sunbeam, the last ray of daylight, raises the somber ocher almost to orange. Here and there small black figures wander around among the tree trunks.

In the above description of a painting entitled *The Garden of Saint-Paul Hospital* (1889), van Gogh refers to five structural elements. Four are what landscape architects today would call hardscape—a gray terrace, a side wall of the house, a stone wall, and stone

A *wooden picket gate similar to several that appear in van Gogh's paintings of flower and vegetable gardens. Here blue morning glories and orange nasturtiums entwine their colors in a blue and orange color harmony.*

RIGHT
Vincent van Gogh,
Pine Trees and Dandelions in the Garden of Saint-Paul Hospital, *detail.*

benches. One is a "softscape" element—a high pine tree whose immense trunks and branches reminded him of a defeated proud man. The rest of his description is devoted to ephemeral color combinations—a yellow pool reflection, ocher-colored pine needles, a yellow and violet sky, black figures.

Although a study of van Gogh's garden paintings and letters shows color to be his most important consideration, almost equal emphasis is given to structure or form—either man-made objects, such as stone walls, reed fences, and gravel paths, or shapes created by plants, particularly trees, such as towering pines and contorted olives. In fact, the most mundane and ordinary objects (particularly in garden scenes) often take on a striking presence in van Gogh's paintings—hay rakes, scythes, wheelbarrows, ladders, and cart wheels.

STRUCTURAL FEATURES

Van Gogh's interest in formal structure—the curve of a path, the arc of a branch—found striking expression in his portrayal of vistas in his paintings. The pronounced lines of perspective that mark his landscape paintings are often produced by structural features—particularly paths, fences, hedges, and walls—and sometimes by a patchwork quilt of fields, flower beds, or vegetable plots. Taking this idea as inspiration, I have created a vista with an exaggerated sense of distance by using a ranch-style fence and a forsythia hedge to present converging lines. The vista leads down to a stream and continues up the other side, the lines bordering a stretch of lawn that progressively narrows, descending the slope and then ascending to end in a green triangle edged by trees. The illusion of immense distance is striking and perfectly captures the imagery of van Gogh's long vistas, as in *Field with Poppies* (1889).

A *chunky wooden bench in a style greatly admired by van Gogh when he stayed at the Asylum of Saint-Paul. Note how the stark simplicity and stolid lines of the bench are in perfect scale to the surroundings, a tapestry garden at Parc Floral des Moutiers, near Varengeville, on the Normandy coast. The founder of the garden,* *Guillaume Mallet, was a collector of Impressionist art. He conceived the idea of a tapestry garden using the foliage of trees and shrubs (and strong textural and structural contrasts) as a result of studying fabrics—drawing conclusions similar to those of van Gogh in his letters explaining his painting* The Garden of the Poets *(1888).*

IN ADDITION TO HIS STRONG SENSITIVITY TO COLOR and form in nature, van Gogh had a tremendous interest in texture—one of the most commonly overlooked elements in a garden. Many books and articles about color in the garden pay such little regard to form and texture (presenting endless examples of using plants for color in beds and borders) that they have caused the eminent garden designer Marco Polo Stufano (director of Wave Hill Garden, New York) to protest that color is the *least* important element for a beautiful garden, behind form and texture.

Van Gogh's interest in texture is exemplified in a painting entitled *Pine Trees and Dandelions in the Garden of Saint-Paul Hospital* (1890). In it the trunks of two mature pine trees provide a beautiful solid, scaly textural quality that contrasts to the frothy white and yellow flower heads of the dandelions that surround it. This painting inspired me to seek trees around the base of which I could plant flowers. Now my garden has several areas that emulate the dandelion painting, one involving an old English walnut circled by pink bleeding hearts and blue woodland phlox. Beneath a mature ash I've planted a collection of 'Barnhaven' primroses in a hot color harmony of red, orange, and yellow. The ash is especially beautiful because radiating out from the base of the trunk is a network of raised roots, the primroses planted between them.

Van Gogh's painting Pine Trees and Dandelions in the Garden of Saint-Paul Hospital *(1890) shows beautiful umbrella pines with deeply fissured bark, surrounded by flowers. In a garden setting, daffodils are a good substitute for dandelions, as seen here.*

Van Gogh's preliminary pen-and-ink sketches of garden scenes—particularly *Fountain in the Garden of Saint-Paul Hospital* (1889)—further illustrate the impact of structural elements in a garden. In this case a circular stone fountain surrounded by the tortured trunks of pine trees is rendered completely without color. Similarly, *Pollarded Willows* (1884), a pen-and-ink sketch that captures an explosion of branches from topknotted willow trees, owes its strength entirely to the form of thick trunks and whiplike branches.

The main purpose of fences in van Gogh's paintings is to produce pronounced lines of perspective, especially from an elevated position. Pickets and reeds are the predominant fence materials in his paintings, occurring mostly in scenes of vegetable gardens and orchards.

Walls serve a similar purpose—to define a space and produce exaggerated lines of perspective. Van Gogh primarily used strong, sturdy walls, although sometimes they have free-flowing lines, as in one of his paintings at Auvers-sur-Oise, *Houses in Auvers* (1890), in which the wall is rendered in beautiful solid detail, complete with peaked capping stones and blocky quarry stones.

Many of van Gogh's garden scenes also feature gates, almost always simple chunky rustic structures made of pickets and latched by a loop of leather.

Paths are another important structural element that van Gogh often featured in his paintings, usually in the form of gravel or meandering footpaths covered with fallen leaves or pine needles. His paths are usually arched over by trees, their branches creating a leaf tunnel. They are often painted in spring, when petals from spent blossoms color the path, as in *Path in the Woods* (1887), or in autumn, when yellow and orange leaves create a similar spontaneous carpeting effect, as in *Les Alyscamps* (1888). In several of the Arles paintings, such as *Public Park at Arles* (1888), the broad sweep of a gravel path is dominant, leading the viewer into the picture through a tunnel of trees. Van Gogh's paintings tend to accentuate the trunks of trees lining his paths, an effect a gardener can achieve by selectively pruning the lower branches of

trees to silhouette their truncated forms, whether pencil straight or contorted.

In my own garden we have connected distinctly different areas by paths, but their materials change from one area to another as they complete a circuit. In the shady sections we generally use pine needles to define the paths. The chestnut-colored mulch is pleasing on the eye and comfortable for strolling, but it changes to gravel in moist areas where drainage is needed to keep the surface dry. We use grass through a "cathedral grove" or leaf tunnel, and laid rough fieldstone for a section of flagstone path through a moist wooded area.

Vincent van Gogh,
Daubigny's Garden, *1890.*
The Rudolf Staechelin
Family Foundation,
Basel, Switzerland.

le jardin de Daubigny

This garden scene resembles Vincent's painting The Stone Bench in the Garden of Saint-Paul Hospital (1889).

RIGHT

Slatted park benches feature in van Gogh's paintings of several French gardens, including Daubigny's Garden (1890). Though van Gogh painted many roses, those in white and pale pink were his favorites.

OPPOSITE

Vincent van Gogh, Daubigny's Garden, detail.

Van Gogh especially liked a path of wheel tracks through a hay field or wheat field, so we have worn similar meandering tracks through wildflower meadows, using an all-terrain vehicle to keep the track well defined.

DECORATIVE FORM

Though van Gogh was most vocal in his liking for certain color contrasts in the garden, his letters and paintings are full of praise for incidental embellishments, such as picket fences, rustic wooden gates, orchard ladders, and even sculptural accents. In letters to Theo he made constant references to garden furnishings, even praising an unusual sculpture: "In a cottage garden I saw a figurehead of a woman carved in wood, from the bow of a Spanish

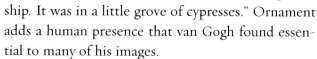

ship. It was in a little grove of cypresses." Ornament adds a human presence that van Gogh found essential to many of his images.

In our own gardens a few incidental artifacts like these cannot only enhance the space but suggest a sense of place and create a recognizable theme more successfully than plants can do alone. For example, a cart wheel propped against a wall suggests the countryside; a ship's figurehead provides a sense of the sea in a sheltered coastal garden; a rustic gate is appropriate for an English-style cottage garden; a Japanese maiden creates an Oriental aura. Van Gogh had an eye for appropriate ornamentation, bringing into focus elements he liked, such as green Versailles planter boxes, rustic gates, and chunky wheelbarrows.

He even eliminated ornamentation that displeased him, like the bulbous terra-cotta urns used throughout the courtyard garden in the hospital at Arles. We know this because in a preliminary ink drawing of the garden the urns are all in place but in his final painting they are totally absent—every one of them deleted—so the garden's clean cart-wheel design and circular pool are more clearly defined.

An analysis of van Gogh's complete works reveals that the following are some of his favorite ornamental structures, with descriptions taken from his letters.

BENCHES. Van Gogh painted the slatted park benches common in French public gardens, but the bench design he seems to have liked the most was found in the garden of the asylum, and several examples of it are still there. A robust piece made from a thick slab of limestone and placed on stone blocks for support, it is evident in numerous paintings of the garden, particularly *The Stone Bench in the Garden of Saint-Paul Hospital* (1889), which shows the chunky stone bench positioned next to a mature umbrella pine and a stone fountain in the background.

BRIDGES. Much of Holland is beneath sea level, with drainage ditches crisscrossing the land, and early in his career van Gogh painted the small footbridges connecting arable fields. When he moved to Paris, he painted railway bridges and road bridges crossing the River Seine. When he moved to Arles, he painted a canal bridge south of town with a drawbridge structure that has become famous as the art world's most recognizable bridge—even more familiar than Monet's canopied, wisteria-covered Japanese bridge. Coincidentally, Monet found the inspiration for his bridge in a Japanese woodblock print by

Hiroshige, who also inspired van Gogh's similar arched bridge in a painting entitled *Japonaiserie: Bridge in the Rain* (1887).

Most of the Impressionists painted bridges as alluring landscape features. Though van Gogh's drawbridge and railway bridges are too big to translate to a garden setting, small versions of his arched Japanese footbridge can be an ideal embellishment. Monet painted his Japanese bridge apple green to harmonize with other green structural elements in his garden, but our own arched Japanese-style bridge is painted rusty red in order to heighten the intense fall leaf color display that occurs every autumn. It also works as part of a monochromatic pink and red color harmony that occurs in spring from the intense flowering of redbud trees and lavender pink azaleas.

COTTAGES. Van Gogh loved humble peasant cottages and wrote about a particular thatched cottage he admired in Holland: "The cottage with its mossy roof reminds me of a wren's nest." He had a special fondness for thatch and painted thatched cottages not only in the countryside of Holland and around Auvers-sur-Oise but also in the Camargue south of Arles. Even in sweeping landscapes of the Alpilles Mountains within sight of the Asylum of Saint-Paul, van Gogh invariably found a humble abode to include as a structural accent and a sign of human presence. One of his most striking images of the resort town of Saintes-Maries-de-la-Mer in the Camargue, entitled *Street in Saintes-Maries* (1888) shows an entire street of thatched cottages, the flowing architectural lines of the snug cottages contrasting sharply with the luxurious growth of a sloping garden. A separate painting of a different location, entitled *The White Cottages* (1888), shows a cluster of similar thatched cottages in a meadow of wild sedge grasses. About this motif van Gogh wrote: "Furthermore, imagine in that landscape which is so

ABOVE
Van Gogh greatly admired the thatched cottages at Saintes-Maries-de-la-Mer, south of Arles, and when he moved back north to Auvers, he wrote how pleased he was to still find thatched cottages, which were fast disappearing in the countryside.

BELOW
A potting shed landscaped to suggest a small cottage similar to the fishermen's huts van Gogh painted at Saintes-Maries-de-la-Mer. He greatly admired cottage gardens, planting a small one at his accommodations near London in 1876, when he worked there as a teacher.

naive, and a good thing too, a cottage whitewashed all over (the roof too) standing in an orange field—certainly orange for the southern sky and the blue Mediterranean provoke an orange tint that gets more intense as the scale of the blue colors gets a more vigorous tone—then the black note of the door, the windows, and the little cross on the ridge of the roof produce a simultaneous contrast of black and white just as pleasing to the eye as blue and orange."

In my garden there are several outbuildings that we have turned into garden accents, including a stone springhouse and a toolshed that once were eyesores. The stone springhouse was roofed in ugly tarpaper, but all that was needed to restore its beauty was to replace the tarpaper with Pennsylvania black slate. A series of kidney-shaped perennial beds were then positioned like a funnel to lead the eye from a sunlit lawn area to the shaded springhouse.

The toolshed had no windows and was clad in ugly white asbestos shingles. However, it bore a vague resemblance to one of van Gogh's "white cottages" of the Camargue. To turn it into a cozy little gardener's cottage like those in his painting, we added windows with window boxes and placed trellises against the shingles so we could train vines up the walls. On one wall where a window was difficult to place, we made a faux window by hanging a mirror in a window frame. The lines of an ugly brick chimney were substantially softened by planting a 'Madame Galen' trumpet vine at the base. This reached six feet the first season, climbing to the top of the chimney by the second and erupting into a pillar of orange trumpet-shaped blooms that are a magnet to hummingbirds.

FOUNTAINS AND WATER FEATURES. A common water feature in parks and gardens throughout France, fountains are most often seen in highly formal settings, often emulating the baroque gardens of Italy. Positioned midway along a formal axis or avenue or at the termination of a vista, they make effective focal points.

The Impressionists as a whole ignored fountains as motifs, and Monet even expressed a dislike for them as garden ornaments. Van Gogh's painting of a circular fountain at the asylum is important in several respects, then, but especially because it is a formal element set in a *woodland* scene. Its stolid architectonic lines contrast powerfully with the sinuous, organic, naturalistic lines of old trees. The fountain appears in several of his paintings of the asylum garden, but it is most clearly shown in an etching entitled *Fountain in the Garden of Saint-Paul Hospital* (1889). During more than thirty years of photographing gardens worldwide, the best example I have seen of a fountain like the one in van Gogh's drawings and paintings is on the grounds of Holker Hall, near Cark-in-Cartmel in the English Lake District. A slightly less ornate circular fountain is seen in van Gogh's paintings of the hospital garden at Arles, although he makes the fountain larger than it is in real life.

Van Gogh's family garden at Nuenen is depicted in two of his paintings, both entitled *The Parsonage Garden at Nuenen with Pond and Figures* (1885), in compositions that can be beautifully emulated today. Both show an autumn scene in which a small pond with a

boat dock is surrounded by trees in brilliant fall foliage, the edges of the pond decorated with clumps of shrubs and ornamental grasses.

Van Gogh's Provençal painting *Les Peiroulets Ravine* (1889) also provides ideas for a water feature. This painting shows two women walking along a rocky path above a pair of waterfalls in a mountainous landscape. Based on this, we have designed a small rock garden featuring two free-form pools and a water cascade, the area planted mostly with ornamental grasses. A small nymph statue pours water into the first pool, which overflows into the second to create the waterfall. The water is recirculated to create a continuous running stream, filling the air with the music of splashing water.

LADDERS. Many of van Gogh's landscapes and gardens feature orchard ladders—sometimes an A-frame ladder that allows the top to be easily poked through tree branches for resting against the trunk. They feature prominently in *Haystacks in Provence* (1888), *Harvest at La Crau* (1888), and *Orchard in Blossom* (1888). Today ladders are the perfect incidental embellishment when it is desirable to create a pastoral feeling. We have permanently propped an A-frame orchard ladder found at a flea market against an old pear tree and planted a bed of 'Barnhaven' primroses around the base. The rough textured trunk of the tree and the lines of the ladder make a good structural contrast, while the primroses—hardy shade-tolerant plants that often grow in English orchards—form a beautiful rust-colored display. Another ladder with conventional straight sides serves as a trellis to train a wisteria vine up into the lofty branches of a mature ash tree. Eventually the ladder will rot away, leaving the coiling vines to be self-supporting. To decorate the base of the ladder, we use 'Barnhaven' primroses in company with daffodils for a red, orange, and yellow hot color harmony.

Vincent van Gogh,
Exterior of a Restaurant
at Asnières, *1887.* Van Gogh
Museum, Amsterdam.

PLANTERS. In his painting *Exterior of a Restaurant at Asnières* (1887), van Gogh depicted a planter brimming with the bright pink blooms of a flowering oleander. The painting was based on a row of six box-shaped planters filled with shrubs that stood outside a Parisian restaurant against a yellow wall with green shutters. Later, in a letter to Theo expressing his desire to plant two oleanders in tubs outside his house in Arles, the idea seems to come from this Asnières painting. A subsequent painting entitled *Vincent's House in Arles (The Yellow House)* (1888) shows similar colors—yellow walls with green shutters.

The wooden boxlike planter he admired is known as the Versailles planter because it was first used at Versailles Palace to grow tender trees like oranges and palms. The original Versailles planters were painted white and placed on casters so they could easily be moved indoors during frosty weather, but Parisians took an immense liking to the square shape.

WHEELS, WAGONS, AND WHEELBARROWS. Van Gogh's gardens and landscapes frequently feature wheels—on wheelbarrows and hay carts, on parked horse-drawn carriages, and on gypsy caravans. *Harvest at La Crau* (1888), for example, places a blue hay cart center stage, and *First Steps* (1889) shows a gardener holding out his arms to embrace a small child, with a wheelbarrow prominent.

Often when designing garden spaces, especially intimate nooks and crannies, the placement of a few incidental props can turn a mundane garden setting into a rustic or romantic one. Small goat carts with wooden wheels and rusty farm cultivators with a metal wheel can be purchased from secondhand stores, the cart to hold potted plants and the cultivator merely to serve as a decorative country accent. Wheels by themselves can also make wonderful embellishments for the garden—not only rusty old metal cart wheels and wooden wagon wheels but also worn millstones.

theme GARDENS

"The little cottage garden, done vertically, has in itself amazing colors; the dahlias are a rich and somber purple, the double row of flowers of the most vivid reddish orange, with yellowish green fruits. The ground gray, the tall reeds, 'canes,' blue-green, the fig trees emerald, the sky blue, the houses white with green windows and red roofs in the morning full of sunshine, in the evening drowned in the shadows thrown by the fig trees and the reeds."

LETTER TO THEO (SUMMER 1888)

Prairie wildflowers, including black-eyed susans, purple sunflowers, calliopsis, and pink bottlebrush, surround a clump of prairie cordgrass in a plant partnership like van Gogh's paintings of flowery meadows.

V AN GOGH PAINTED both formal and informal gardens in a range of locations and climate zones. The gardens he painted in Holland, Paris, and Auvers-sur-Oise experience a harsher climate than in Arles, Saintes-Maries-de-la-Mer, and Saint-Rémy, which are in the South of France and influenced by the temperate Mediterranean Sea. Frosts along the coast are infrequent or light. The geological differences between north and south are also profound—ranging from the flat, predominantly sandy terrain of Holland to the rugged, flinty soil of the Alpilles Mountains of Provence, where the artist was delighted to discover vineyards.

Van Gogh adored extremes, from the clear, saturated light of the Mediterranean to star-spangled nightscapes. He loved the sea with its tossing waves, the pastoral beauty he discovered along country roads, woodland with undergrowth, and rocky outcrops with pines twisted by the mistral wind, resembling the windswept pines of Japanese woodblock prints. He admired starburst effects, like the cart-wheel design of the courtyard garden in the grounds of the hospital at Arles; he preferred massed color, like that of the cutting garden near Arles; he delighted in finding checkerboard patterns formed by blocks of vegetables, or agricultural fields defined by walls, hedgerows, and fences; and he was inspired by gardens with good foliage contrasts, where the shapes and textures of trees and shrubs were more important than riotous color.

While many of van Gogh's subjects (like the vegetable plots of Montmartre and the Peiroulets Ravine in Provence) are on a scale too large for the average home garden, others can be adapted without much change or stretch of the imagination. From his letters and paintings it is possible to extrapolate the most important garden elements to create well-defined garden designs on at least ten stimulating themes.

VAN GOGH'S ORANGE AND BLACK GARDEN

One of van Gogh's most unusual planting ideas was the coupling of orange and black, which he first discovered in two small cottage gardens in Arles and rendered in several paintings, notably *Garden Behind a House* (1888). The orange in this garden is mostly from African marigolds, while the black is mostly from dark maroon nasturtiums. In another garden that he painted, the orange elements are again mostly from African marigolds, but the black is from a black scabiosa.

I had long been interested in bringing van Gogh's orange and black garden to life, and when I shared my thoughts with New Zealand garden writer Olive Dunn, I suggested she might like to take up the challenge herself. After some initial trepidation, she agreed, and so independently we created different small-space designs during one summer.

"What surprises and thunderbolts tip out of the mail sometimes," she wrote, describing her initial response in her monthly garden column. "When the post brought

a letter from Derek Fell late last year confirming that he would be in New Zealand in January, I was delighted until I read further. Would I plant an orange and black garden for his next book on van Gogh?"

In the May 1994 issue of the *New Zealand Gardener,* Dunn went on to describe her reservations: "Total shock is an understatement of my reaction. The very thought of orange and black in my largely pastel gardens was almost sacrilege. I really felt it was stretching my color sensitivity a little too far. For a time even my dreams seemed to be haunted by sunflowers that got bigger and bigger, and black pansies and nasturtiums running amok everywhere."

Dunn expressed precisely the reaction of many women I discussed the idea with—complete apprehension. Men tended to warm to the idea immediately. Black and orange! But how would it be possible when there are so few black flowers to use and orange is such an overpowering color? Dunn explained how she eventually set aside her fears and decided to give the garden a try: "Even my friends were rather stunned, and concerned as to where I was going to plant this garden. Some suggested over the fence in my brother's garden and one friend even quipped that perhaps garden visitors would mistakenly read it as a sign of some aberration, like Van Gogh eventually suffered.

"All thought of refusing was offset by the fun of a new challenge," she explained. So she set to work assembling the components, disappointed that because of the lateness of the season she could not use black irises and black tulips, which she adores. Instead, she selected plants that could bloom in summer. The orange elements were easy to obtain—'Golden Gem' marigolds, orange tiger lilies, California poppies, 'Andries Orange' dahlias, 'Jewel' nasturtiums, and 'Moorheim Beauty' heleniums.

The black elements were more difficult, but a fine array of foliage and flowers finally asserted the essential black tones. They included a background of bronze-leaf fennel, an edging of black mondo grass and black pansies, black carnations and black columbine, even black hollyhocks. The striking black central discs of 'Floristan' sunflowers, calendulas, heleniums, and gloriosa daisies also peppered the planting with black accents.

Van Gogh's black and orange garden can be done predominantly with annuals, but I find the best result comes when annuals and perennials are combined, especially with Asiatic lilies used for splashes of yellow, orange, and red, and gloriosa daisies for their bold black centers.

Dunn reported that the most surprising result of this whole stimulating exercise was the agreeable response from garden visitors. Rather than being shocked, they found the orange and black planting a pleasant surprise. One man commented that it was "an aesthetic bombshell," particularly in a garden otherwise so washed in pastel. "A man's color," he called it.

The biggest lessons here are that orange does need careful toning with different hues and softening foliage and that small pockets of vibrant colors can bring excitement to the garden. Dunn was reminded of a quote by Sir Joshua Reynolds, who once advised her florist students: "Don't condemn a thing today; tomorrow you might have learned to appreciate it."

VAN GOGH'S CUTTING GARDEN

Of all the gardens van Gogh painted, the most colorful are a farm garden and a cottage garden on the outskirts of Arles. They are what we would today call "cutting gardens," for they are planted with mostly long-stemmed annuals in color blocks accessible for cutting to provide floral arrangements for the house. These gardens stimulated in him much comment and analysis, especially in his correspondence to Wilhelmien in the summer of 1888 in which he suggested to her plants that would produce the same color themes in the family's garden in Holland (see page 45).

The farm garden was shown to van Gogh by Joseph Roulin, a postman he befriended who knew the region intimately from delivering mail. Van Gogh

(see page 45)

RIGHT
Vincent van Gogh,
The Garden at Arles, *1888.*
Haags Gemeentemuseum,
Netherlands.

Overall view of a cottage garden on a misty morning, showing how pinpricks of white not only produce a glittering appearance but also help to harmonize the predominantly yellow and pink petal colors.

described this painting to his sister as his most elaborate composition. At first glance it appears mostly a hot study of red, orange, and yellow, predominantly from marigolds and geraniums, with contrasts of blue from love-in-a-mist. But closer inspection shows important touches of black from maroon nasturtiums and a maroon scabiosa—both of which he rendered jet black. Branches of shrubs in the background

along with shadows of cypress and fig foliage are also rendered in black; indeed, every portion of the canvas presents a different one of van Gogh's favorite color harmonies, including black and orange, black and white, yellow and blue, and red and green. He made two studies in oils of the farm garden, the first a vertical view entitled *Flowering Garden* (1888), which is a close-up study with the flowers almost bleeding off the edges of the frame. He also painted a horizontal, overall view showing a path running diagonally through the garden plot. Van Gogh's favorite

color harmonies are so clearly evident that one wonders if they were planted that way by the farmer's wife, or whether he took artistic license to arrange the plants so they made the partnerships he desired. Fortunately, he rendered a detailed pen-and-ink of the garden before painting the scene, which indicates that he took little artistic license.

A few days later he encountered a similar cutting garden behind a cottage attached to a bathing establishment. In his painting he used the same color harmonies to convey its brilliancy—this time from mostly

LEFT

This cutting garden—inspired by van Gogh's vibrant painting Flowering Garden with Path (1888), which shows a farm wife's cutting garden near Arles—features mostly red, orange, and yellow in a hot color harmony, with spots of black and blue for contrasts.

RIGHT

Vincent van Gogh, Memory of the Garden at Etten, detail of dahlias, marigolds, and geraniums.

marigolds and dahlias. Black contrasts represent what appear to be maroon scabiosa. This painting, entitled *Garden Behind a House* (1888), was also preceded by a detailed pen-and-ink sketch entitled *A Garden with Flowers* (1888); this also suggests that he changed little when he applied paint to canvas, merely exaggerating certain colors to better present his chosen harmonies.

In my garden we have created a cutting garden inspired by the farm garden paintings, a rectangle of space dissected by a path just like the one seen in van Gogh's work. Figs, junipers, and oleander bushes are important background components in his painting, and we are fortunate to have a contorted English walnut, a spreading sugar maple, and spire-shaped junipers. The space is always planted in the same color harmonies and usually undergoes three transformations in a season: pansies and foxgloves form the main focus in spring, marigolds and nasturtiums in summer, and chrysanthemums with cosmos in autumn.

The path running through the garden is flagstone. We chose rough fieldstone for the pavers so creeping plants like alyssum and thyme can grow between the cracks. The path contrasts with a yew hedge to define the space and provide strong lines of perspective. The garden provides armloads of fresh flowers for the house from spring through autumn.

VAN GOGH'S VEGETABLE GARDEN

Though van Gogh's paintings of flower gardens are better known because of their vibrant colors, he painted a large number of plots containing vegetables and fruit trees. These almost always feature pronounced lines of perspective, created not only by the fences, walls, ditches, and hedgerows used to define the spaces but also by the different colors of vegetables planted in blocks, with lettuce rendered as a yellow-green next to cabbages painted blue-green and onions represented by an emerald green.

Within view of van Gogh's bedroom window at the asylum was a stout stone wall erected to cushion the force of the mistral wind. Stone walls may have reminded him of his father's walled parsonage garden at Nuenen, but in his paintings they also serve to define spaces and produce the strong lines of perspective he always sought.

It should also be noted how authentic van Gogh tried to be when capturing the dynamics of a particular cultivated plot. The way he spaced trees in the olive and peach orchards is true to nature, not telescoped together as Monet might have done, and his representations of pruned trees such as apricots and pears are so accurate in their essential structure that Professor Robert Gutowski of the Morris Arboretum in Philadelphia uses posters of the paintings to teach his students correct pruning techniques.

In designing our own small-space vegetable garden, the first consideration was a decorative low stone wall to define the space. On the outside perimeter of the wall we have planted peonies for decorative effect. Within the wall we grow vegetables in blocks rather than regimented straight rows, which

Though rainbow-colored chard is a recent breeding achievement, it is used decoratively here to acknowledge van Gogh's paintings of cultivated spaces. Silver sage and golden oregano are colorful herbs planted in tile pots to provide textural contrasts with the chard.

produces an attractive quilt design found in van Gogh's Montmartre paintings. Contrasting varieties of vegetables are deliberately planted to make the quilt pattern within the constraints of a largely green motif. For example, the lime green variety of lettuce known as 'Australian Yellow' is planted beside the bronze-leaf foliage of 'Red Sails'. Blue-green cabbages and dark green spinach are also used in an early spring planting. Walkways between the plots are mulched with yellow straw.

RIGHT

Twilight garden with the moon rising above an island bed of white flowers and a white trellised arch.

FAR RIGHT

A white garden featuring 'Purity' climbing roses, Marguerite daisies, and a silvery edging of gray lavender cotton, perfect for enjoying in the moonlight.

BELOW

A white garden featuring 'Iceberg' roses, mock orange, and snow-in-summer. All-white gardens like this can remind us of van Gogh's Starry Night (1889) and other nightscapes he painted.

VAN GOGH'S TWILIGHT GARDEN

No one among the Impressionist artists captured the allure of nightscapes more successfully than van Gogh. His *Night Café* (1888), *Starry Night over the Rhone* (1888), and *Starry Night at Saint-Rémy* (1889) are examples of his genius for finding colors in the dark of night. Many of his canvases, such as *Twilight Before the Storm, Montmartre* (1887) and *Olive Grove* (1889), evoke the special sensations of twilight.

Our twilight garden, inspired by van Gogh's *Starry Night at Saint-Rémy* (1889), includes a white arch to frame the moon as it climbs the sky above a distant row of trees. The plantings are predominantly white because pale colors have a special luminosity in moonlight. Some important tree silhouettes provide dark backgrounds for structural effects—like the silhouetted tree forms in van Gogh's painting. These include a pair of billowing evergreen American boxwoods, which have a looser habit and faster growth than English boxwoods (allowing clematis and moonflower vines to scramble through their branches), and a pair of spire-shaped junipers with silvery blue foliage.

Low-growing annuals, such as petunias, datura, and sweet alyssum provide a reflective carpeting effect, while biennial white foxgloves, perennial astilbes, early summer phlox, and perennial snakeroot produce spires of white or cream-colored flowers. White daisies—especially the ox-eye daisy, Shasta daisy, and chamomile daisy—are important for intermediate height. White vining moonflower, a white climbing rose such as 'Iceberg,' and white clematis vines carry reflective blossoms high above the limits of other plants, even over the white arch.

Silvery gray foliage from artemisia and lamb's ears is as important as white flowers for tonal values, while the lustrous lime green foliage of 'Royal Standard' hosta positively shines at twilight with perfumed white flowers. Fragrant white waterlilies float on the surface of a circular pool, strategically placed to capture the moon's reflection.

A white garden with silvery accents not only provides a restful refuge at the end of a hot summer's day but is sensational in moonlight, and the selection of flowers is almost limitless since there is hardly a plant family in cultivation that does not include white, cream, pale yellow, or pale pink in its color range—all suitable for reflecting the silvery glow of moonlight.

**V**incent van Gogh, Olive Trees, 1889. The Minneapolis Institute of Arts, the William Hood Dunwoody Fund, Minneapolis, Minnesota.

VAN GOGH'S TAPESTRY GARDEN

Van Gogh completed a total of four paintings entitled *The Garden of the Poets* and rendered another seven with different titles, for a total of eleven paintings of the same garden. The garden itself was predominantly planted with shrubs and trees to create a tapestry garden emphasizing form and texture, with subtle color coming mostly from foliage contrasts. Only the asylum garden at Saint-Rémy was painted more often than the poets' garden.

One of the poets' garden paintings is entitled *Public Park with Weeping Willows* (1888), and it shows a

mature weeping willow among other trees, including billowing oleanders, cushion-shaped cypresses, and tapered evergreen junipers. I am fortunate to have a beautiful mature weeping willow beside a stream, and so we decided to make it the central element in a tapestry garden similar to van Gogh's poets' garden. While his garden was in a flat area, the site we chose sloped up from a stream and pond, allowing a better presentation of the foliage contrasts. These include not only the stupendous willow but also a weeping cherry, several billowing Russian olives with silvery leaves, spirelike junipers with dark green leaves, a vigorous clump of variegated maiden grass, and a carpet of leathery green hellebores, among other perennial or woody plants. There is a particular spot, on the opposite slope, where the branches of a sugar maple help to frame the tapestry garden. Here we have placed a slatted bench, the better to view the soothing panorama of shapes, textures, and foliage effects.

OPPOSITE

In this tapestry garden at Le Vasterival, located along the Normandy coast, Princess Greta Sturdza creates effects inspired by van Gogh's paintings. The creamy yellow of Norway maple leaves and the orange of Mollis azaleas in the background are colors that go well together. The strong, dark, vertical line of the trunk and the radiating pattern of dark branches against the lighter yellow and orange create the type of contrast that van Gogh sought in the landscape.

LEFT

Vincent van Gogh, The Garden of the Poets, *detail.*

ABOVE

Example of a beautiful tapestry garden using evergreens to create a weave of mostly green tones, similar to the one in van Gogh's The Garden of the Poets (1888). Note how this soothing garden space is built up with three levels of color—low, spreading groundcovers featuring clumps of heather and 'Blue Rug' juniper; medium-height cone-shaped gold-leaf cypress; and a background of tall green spruce.

VAN GOGH'S CART-WHEEL GARDEN

After van Gogh painted the courtyard garden in the hospital at Arles, he wrote that the courtyard's blue and yellow archways reminded him of a Moorish palace and the design suggested a pendant. At the center of the pendant was a circular pool with goldfish, and narrow paths radiated out like the spokes of a wheel to create pie-shaped beds. Though the property survives with the arches and garden largely intact, it is no longer a hospital but a crafts center within walking distance of the town hall.

Van Gogh named the flowers he saw in the garden and made special reference to groundcovers of hellebore, edgings of sweet violet, and beds of ranunculus and boxwood topiary. Today the garden is planted in a similar color scheme, usually with summer bedding plants to re-create Vincent's painting.

Translating these ideas for a home garden, we have used the pendant design for a beautiful small-space herb garden. Brick paths define four planting sections (each dissected by a miniature boxwood hedge), while a sundial makes a central focal point in place of the pool. Instead of violas to edge the beds, we use chives, and when they bloom in early spring the effect is especially lovely.

LEFT

The concept of a cart-wheel design can be applied to a much smaller scale than in van Gogh's courtyard garden. Here a similar design is used for a decorative herb garden, the paths edged with chives.

RIGHT

High-elevation view of the courtyard garden at the Arles hospital prior to planting, showing the design. Featuring a fountain and goldfish pool at its center, it has paths radiating out like the spokes of a wheel in a highly formal layout. The beds are edged in violets. This view reminded van Gogh of a Moorish garden with its golden arches.

VAN GOGH'S ROCK GARDEN

Montmajour, a region of farmland north of Arles, is sandwiched between the Alpilles Mountains and the flatlands of the Rhone estuary—the Camargue. Fertile fields of wheat stretch out like golden carpets in summer, penetrated by roads that run as straight as a gunbarrel, the pristine landscape interrupted by hummocks of limestone; cushions of herbs and heath grow among the weatherworn boulders. Lone pine trees bent by the mistral wind etch the sky with stunted, writhing branches, bringing to mind Japanese bonsai trees. Van Gogh admired these outcrops of stark, rugged beauty and portrayed them as rock gardens.

Unlike Monet, who disliked rocks and statuary in gardens, van Gogh—if he had been able to make a garden of his own—might have planted a rock garden to resemble his painting *Rocks with Oak Tree* (1888). He painted two other motifs that portray natural rock gardens. *Les Peiroulets Ravine* (1889) shows two women walking a rocky trail between waterfalls, and *Entrance to a Quarry near Saint-Rémy* (1889) presents a grottolike cavern where Roman slaves once quarried limestone.

When we decided to make a rock garden, I was intent on *not* having the fuss and bother of an English rock garden, traditionally planted with finicky alpine plants that need constant weeding and coddling. I favored something more rugged and easy to care for, as shown in van Gogh's bold paintings, and the design that evolved from studying his art and letters is a gem consisting of two pools that spill water one into the other, surrounded by rough fieldstone rocks, a perfect miniature of *Les Peiroulets Ravine* (1889).

VAN GOGH'S GRASS GARDEN

Van Gogh had an astute appreciation of grasses, and he painted them up close, mixing the starburst blades of sedge grasses with the sparkle of wildflowers, and also from afar, showing vast sweeps of wheat disappearing to the horizon. His interest in grasses strengthened after reading *Leaves of Grass* by the American poet Walt Whitman, in which Whitman declared that a blade of grass was no less impressive than the motions of the stars. Whitman suggested that an artist could do worse than consider leaves of grass, and that appears to have been the impetus behind many of van Gogh's close views of grasses. In *Wheat Field with Lark* (1887) he captured the sensation of the wind blowing through the arched leaf blades of green and beige grasses dotted with sapphire blue cornflowers and blood red poppies.

Most of us can't have our own wheat fields, of course, but a meadow or hay field can create a similar effect. Ours becomes spangled with meadow grasses through all the seasons—blue-eyed grass and white ox-eye daisies in spring, yellow hawkweed and Queen Anne's lace in summer, yellow swamp sunflowers and

purple ironweed in autumn. Whenever I see a plant partnership starting naturally, I help it along by seeding or transplanting more of the same so the meadow colors are constantly changing. We also use grasses in our sunny perennial beds to soothe the stiffness of perennials like pink joe-pye weed, red beebalm, and stonecrop sedums. A long, wide perennial border edging the field acts as a transition between the cultivated garden and the wild meadow.

Best of all, we have planted several special grass gardens along the sunny banks of our stream, mixing clump-forming kinds like fountain grass with spreading kinds like ribbon grass. A particularly beautiful planting contrasts the grass blades with the sweeping stems of a weeping willow. The play of greens is enchanting enough in summer but becomes even more beautiful in autumn as the grasses flower profusely and change to amber tones.

VAN GOGH'S POND

As we know from van Gogh's paintings, his family's parsonage garden at Nuenen was a beautiful space, complete with a pond, a wooden boat dock, and pondside plantings of ornamental grasses, birch trees, and shrubs.

Like van Gogh's pond at Nuenen, our own is small—dug out originally to provide a watering hole for livestock when the property was a Mennonite dairy farm. It is fed by a small stream and has a dam with a spillway. When I acquired the property, the pond was badly silted and had no pondside plantings whatsoever, not even a daffodil, and it begged to be embellished with vegetation. Muskrats were living in the sides, and they had undermined the spillway, so that the pond level sank quickly during dry spells.

Before I began planting, the sides were proofed against muskrats by repairing the dam and laying a chain-link fence flat against the sides. During a severe summer drought prior to the rat-proofing, the pond dried up, and so I dug out the silt by hand, using some of it to grade around the pond. The first plants to be put in place were some azaleas planted in a broad brushstroke up a slope. Then some 'Heritage' river birches were added to provide tall, leafy surrounding elements, and some variegated miscanthus grass, flag irises, Japanese water irises, daylilies, astilbes, hostas, and daffodils were planted as transitional elements between the water and the higher ground. Plant partnerships were aimed for—blue with yellow water irises; red cardinal flowers with silvery miscanthus grass; heart-shaped velvety leaves of giant coltsfoot among the pale birch trunks that reflect the colors of sunrises and sunsets; yellow perennial foxgloves and blue sage; yellow black-eyed Susans and crimson hardy hibiscus. Floating plants like waterlilies and parrot's feather decorate the surface of the pond.

With clumps of maiden grass and birch trees on its banks, this pond is similar in appearance to one that van Gogh painted several times in his father's parsonage garden.

OPPOSITE

This secluded shade garden was
planted to reflect van Gogh's painting
Two Figures in a Landscape
(1889), which shows a couple walking
through poplar trees underplanted
with yellow buttercups and white
ox-eye daisies. Instead of poplars, the
decorative trunks in this painting
belong to 'Heritage' river birches. The
white and yellow flowers are mostly
golden coreopsis and Shasta daisies.

BELOW

This woodland garden featuring
a slab bench and ivy-girdled tree
is similar to the asylum garden at
Saint-Rémy, where van Gogh was
comforted by the bowers of greenery.

RIGHT

Vincent van Gogh,
Undergrowth with Two
Figures, detail of wildflowers.

The crowning ornamental touch was a rusty red boat dock that served as a place for children to fish and gain access to the iced-over surface for skating in winter. The pond never did acquire the grandeur of Monet's water garden, on which I originally based my design, mostly because of size restrictions, but after the boat dock was in place, I chanced upon van Gogh's painting *The Parsonage Garden at Nuenen with Pond and Figures* (1885), and I was astonished at the uncanny resemblance.

VAN GOGH'S SHADE GARDENS

Van Gogh was drawn to woodlands from the moment he took up painting, and his shade gardens present a wealth of ideas for tranquil designs. In Holland he painted avenues of trees, the towering trunks of poplars stabbing into the sky and creating strong lines of perspective in green or gold, depending on the season. In Paris he found woodland paths winding through tunnels of ivy-girdled trees, portions of the paths in spring colored by the fallen petals of lilacs, chestnuts, or redbuds. In Arles he chose a high elevation to paint an avenue of poplars in autumn, so the trunks of the poplars stand out in stark contrast to a path covered in golden leaves. And in Saint-Rémy he found the eerie asylum garden full of shady nooks and crannies, arched over by tall umbrella pines with scaly trunks and needles that turned the woodland floor ocher in winter.

Though some of van Gogh's asylum paintings reflect his melancholy moods, many have a magical, almost supernatural aura about them. The flowery aspects of some probably did not reflect the rather bleak reality of unkempt lawns and high, prisonlike walls. Rather, van Gogh often imbued the severe, cloistered buildings with the splendor of a stately home, evoking an atmosphere as alluring and serene as the poets' garden.

The lesson van Gogh teaches repeatedly in these and other woodland paintings is the visual beauty of "carpeting effects," when fallen petals or leaves paint the woodland floor as vibrantly as a massed planting of flowers. Perhaps the most unusual and striking painting of all is of a woodland in Auvers where flowering plants create this effect. Entitled *Two Figures in a Landscape* (1890), the painting shows regimental rows of poplar trees underplanted with a riot of shimmering flowers—seemingly white feverfew and yellow buttercups that one would not normally associate with a shade garden. Initially one wonders how it is possible to have meadow flowers blooming so freely in a woodland. The answer lies in the choice of tree. Poplars have small, flickering leaves that admit more light than such trees as maples and oaks, and their branches hug the trunk, so a close spacing of poplars would still admit sufficient light for buttercups and feverfew to flower.

Poplars can be problematic trees, however, because they are brittle and tend to be short-lived.

In autumn a grove of 'Heritage' river birches turns golden yellow, carpeting the ground with leaves and reminding us of

Les Alyscamps (1888), van Gogh's painting of a public park in Arles where avenues of poplars create a carpeting effect.

While van Gogh could take artistic license and improve the color of their trunks, the dull gray of poplar bark is not ideal for ornamental effect in a garden. In van Gogh's painting, however, the poplar grove is backed by a grove of dark evergreens, the better for the poplar trunks to stand out.

After careful consideration I decided to use river birches in my own garden rather than poplars—not the usual river birch (*Betula nigra*) but the special selection known as 'Heritage'. It has the advantage of honey-colored bark from the tip of the tree to the soil line, whereas the wild species shows the ornamental coloration only at the tip of the tree. Another advantage of 'Heritage' is its fast growth. I also wanted an evergreen background and would have preferred hemlocks, but they are too slow-growing. So I settled on dawn redwoods (*Metasequoia gyptostroboides*).

Normally, a river birch will grow branches all the way to the ground and sometimes produce multiple trunks. I wanted long, straight trunks like those in van Gogh's painting, and so I trimmed away all the lower branches, the better to emphasize the decorative bark. Moreover, the leafy growth of the river birch is not dense but light and airy, like that of a poplar, and when planted an even ten feet apart and pruned of their lower branches, the trees still allow sufficient light to penetrate for meadow grasses like ox-eye daisies and swamp sunflowers to flower.

Our shade gardens in other areas also have van Gogh touches—ivy-girdled trees along a path where tree branches arch high overhead to create a cathedral effect; trees trimmed of lower branches to emphasize sinuous trunks and a lush canopy; English primroses planted among tree roots; pine needles used as a mulch along portions of a winding path; shredded leaves used for mulching flower beds where clumps of white feverfew produce billowing masses of white flowers like foaming surf; ghostly white arums and hellebores with nodding cup-shaped flowers in the darkest recesses; stone walls coated with moss and algae.

Van Gogh was tireless in his search for powerful images, never vacillating or indecisive in his choice of subjects. He studied his motifs carefully, often rendering them first as sketches before painting them, and deliberating for long periods on precisely how to capture the beauty of a particular plant or garden. Once he decided on a composition, he was clear in his mind about what he wanted to show and he worked quickly, often completing a canvas in an hour. Writing to fellow painter Emile Bernard, he explained his technique: "My brushstroke has no system at all. I hit the canvas with irregular touches of the brush, which I leave as they are. Patches of thickly laid-on color, spots of canvas left uncovered, here and there portions that are left absolutely unfinished, repetitions, savageries; in short, I am inclined to think that the result is disquieting and irritating as to be a godsend to those people who have fixed, preconceived ideas about technique."

This manner of working—spending hours and days anguishing over a scene and then attacking the canvas with such purpose and intensity—explains why his landscape motifs are so powerful and memorable when used as inspiration for garden designs. And most of the time, while painting, he was extremely happy. "I work in the middle of the day, in the full sunshine, without any shadow at all, in the wheat fields," he told Theo, "and I enjoy it like a cicada."

A *meadow garden planted in a style that resembles many of van Gogh's paintings of wildflower gardens, both in Provence and at Auvers in the countryside north of Paris. Included in the mixture of annuals and perennials are gloriosa daisies, Asiatic lilies, daylilies, and ox-eye daisies.*

B O U Q U E T S

"*Many people here like him . . . he has friends who send him every week a lot of beautiful flowers that he uses for still lifes. He paints chiefly flowers, especially to make the colors of his next pictures brighter and clearer.*"

LETTER FROM THEO IN PARIS TO VAN GOGH'S MOTHER,
DISCUSSING HER SON VINCENT (SUMMER 1886)

A *primrose garden planted around the roots of an ash tree, with colors chosen to produce a hot color harmony. A small table bouquet made fresh from the garden echoes the type of hot color harmony van Gogh liked to paint in still life arrangements.*

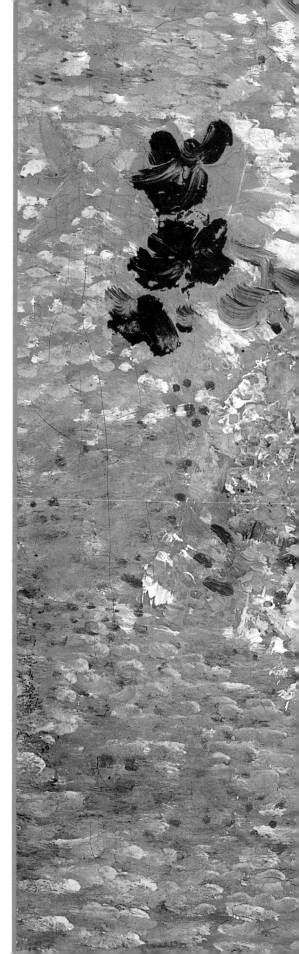

THE THREE GREATEST PAINTERS of the Impressionist era—Renoir, Monet, and van Gogh—all painted flowers as still life arrangements, but they did so for different reasons. Renoir especially loved roses. In his teens he painted swags of roses and garlands of roses while working for a porcelain manufacturer in Paris, decorating plates, bowls, and lamp bases to augment the family's income. When he established a home and garden near Nice, he had a rose garden and hardly ever started his day without dashing off a quick vignette of roses picked fresh from the garden and arranged into a simple bouquet. The roses, he explained, were experiments in color values, for he saw in them the flesh tones of the children and women he loved to paint. Look at any Renoir portrait painting and you will see a distinctly rosy glow, with roses often embellishing the hair and hats of his subjects and used as table decorations.

Monet wrote that he originally created his famous Giverny garden "so as to harvest a few flowers to paint when the weather is bad." Only later did he start planting it more ambitiously as a subject to paint. He loved to see every room of his house filled with fragrant flowers, and he valued peonies so highly that he used them as long perennial hedges to outline each plot of vegetables in his 2½-acre kitchen garden, ensuring armloads of blossoms for fragrant floral arrangements in the house.

Unlike Renoir, who sought more subtle tonal effects from his experiments with flowers, van Gogh painted bouquets of flowers as experiments in dramatic color contrasts. During his ten years as an artist, he painted floral arrangements more than any other subject. When he moved to Paris and discovered the radiant beauty of Impressionism, he spent months using floral bouquets repeatedly to lighten his palette and make his paintings glow. During this period he completed

He would use a bulbous vase with a narrow neck when he desired a fanned-out display and a narrow, tall container for an erect, upright arrangement. The color of the container either echoed or complemented the flowers or background color. He carefully selected backgrounds to complement the petal colors, sometimes painting the same subject several times to show a different color contrast, changing only the background. Unlike professional floral arrangers who often design an arrangement to complement a scene, such as a bay window or a foyer, van Gogh for the most part gave no hint of location in his backgrounds, the better to provide dramatic contrasts for his chosen floral subject, whether pink roses, blue irises, or golden sunflowers.

After finishing two paintings of roses and irises in vases, he explained to Theo:

I am doing a canvas of roses with a light green background and two canvases representing two big bunches of irises, one lot against a pink background in which the effect is soft and harmonious because of the combination of greens, pinks, violets. On the other hand, the other, violet bunch (ranging from carmine to pure Prussian blue) stands out against a startling citron background, with other yellow tones in the vase and the stand on which it rests, so it is an effect of tremendously disparate complementaries, which strengthen each other by their juxtaposition.

Van Gogh's most admired floral series involves sunflowers. He began it for the express purpose of using the paintings as room decorations, in anticipation of a visit to Arles from Gauguin. As he wrote Theo: "I am thinking of decorating my studio with half a dozen pictures of 'Sunflowers,' a decoration in which the raw or broken chrome yellows will blaze forth on various backgrounds—blue, from the palest malachite green to royal blue, framed in thin strips of wood painted with orange lead."

The sunflower series shows two kinds of flowers— singles (with one layer of petals) and doubles (with

more than forty floral bouquets in his resolve to excel at color, stating emphatically: "I have made myself a series of color studies . . . seeking oppositions of blue and orange, red and green, yellow and violet, seeking *les tons rompus et neutres* [broken and neutral tones] to harmonize brutal extremes."

Though van Gogh's main focus is color impact, his choice of containers is crucial to the overall designs he painted, both for color and shape. Writing to Theo about his first meeting with Dr. Gachet, he expressed reservations about being too friendly with the doctor, but was pleased at the large number of vases for arrangements the doctor had available: "His house is full, full like an antique dealer's, of things that are not always interesting. But nevertheless there is this advantage, there is always something for arranging flowers in or for a still life."

LEFT

An informal arrangement of sunflowers embodies the power and energy of van Gogh's series of sunflower paintings, some in monochromatic compositions and others in complementary color harmonies involving blue as the background. The thick impasto application of paint to capture the brilliance of sunflower petals on canvas was inspired by a painting of peonies by Eduard Manet.

OPPOSITE

Vincent van Gogh, Sunflowers, 1888. National Gallery, London.

PAGES 134–35

Vincent van Gogh, Sunflowers, *detail.*

*V*an Gogh liked gladiolus for their spiky flower clusters, and he painted them repeatedly in arrangements. In letters he described how the stems would automatically splay out like a fan when placed in a vase, as seen here in an outdoor display.

A simple arrangement of pansies, inspired by van Gogh's painting entitled Tambourine with Pansies (1886), uses a circular tile in place of the tambourine.

multiple layers forming a dome)—without any fill or accent material. Some of the arrangements feature both kinds. Van Gogh was inspired to arrange sunflowers this way after seeing a painting by Manet of a peony arrangement in which Manet used a heavy impasto application of pink and red, with the raised edges of his brush and palette knife providing minimal modeling for the petals.

Van Gogh's heavy impasto brushwork intentionally presents the sunflowers as burning suns. Some have black centers, which generate the black and orange contrast he had recently discovered in a cutting garden.

In the early 1930s, when the great British floral arranger Constance Spry began formulating guidelines and rules in order to teach flower arranging as an art form—with words such as *structure, style, form, balance, harmony,* and *rhythm* to explain concepts of floral art—she studied the work of great painters. How much she learned from van Gogh's art is not known, but the sheer volume of his work and the lessons that can be learned from his carefully conceived floral still lifes could fill a book, for he took inspiration not only from the Dutch genre masters and Japanese woodblock artists but also from the still life arrangements of the early French Impressionists—pointedly referring to an arrangement of sunflowers by Monet and the peonies by Manet as sources of inspiration.

It must be remembered, however, that van Gogh arranged flowers in order to paint them, not necessarily to use for household decoration. Many of his flower choices, such as corn poppies and irises, are short-lived in arrangements. His glorious painting of orange crown imperials in a bulbous, gleaming copper vase against a violet background would probably earn few accolades in an awards competition because the cut stems would pervade the room with the odor of skunk! However, when gardeners have an abundance of flowers during the growing season, they pay little regard to longevity and enjoy using short-lived flowers as van Gogh did.

Nevertheless, the most important design elements in van Gogh's floral still life paintings teach the basics of floral design—color, structure, texture, and location. He considered color paramount, particularly quiet or brutal contrasts (most noticeable in his iris arrangements) or strong monochromatic statements (as in some of his sunflower series).

Structure is evident in his choice of flowers—often spirelike plants such as hollyhocks and gladiolus, which create a tall triangular pattern, or low spreading plants

A *mixture of black and white hollyhocks plus white phlox, white astilbes, and white feverfew is arranged to produce a startling black and white color contrast, which van Gogh described as an evocative color combination.*

such as pansies, which make a horizontal design. He often created a starburst effect by splaying out flower stems to make a fan, and occasionally introduced cascading plants like grasses and lilacs to soften the lines of stiffer-stemmed flowers. His choice of container added not only an important structural quality in many cases but also textural contrast. I especially like his use of an earthy terra-cotta urn to display a collection of wayside wildflowers in *Poppies and Daisies* (1890), which also includes some wispy grasses and blue cornflowers.

Also significant is his use of a circular clear glass container to display a single stem of almond blossoms in *Blossoming Almond Branch in Glass* (1888). The smooth lines of the container and the sharply angled branch studded with plump buds are a perfect example of Japanese ikebana, which highly values minimalism.

In the main, van Gogh's arrangements are what we would call country style, using mostly common garden flowers massed in one type or grouped with other flowers chosen mostly for their color and form. Some backgrounds show a wallpaper design, indicating a living room or parlor, but probably because van Gogh lived in spartan surroundings, little else is evident.

It should also be noted that in van Gogh's day, flowers in a container were generally held in place by the volume of stems, and so it was generally desirable to fill the neck of the vase or container with the maximum number of stems it would hold. With narrow-necked containers, stems would fall into position by gravity; heavier-stemmed flowers such as irises would splay out like a fan to the sides, while thin, long-stemmed flowers like cornflowers would hold in place better within a tall, wide-mouthed vase. In the Impressionist era there was no such product as Oasis—the firm, green, spongelike material that is used extensively by professional flower arrangers today to hold flower stems firmly in position.

This arrangement of branches forced into flowers includes pink quince, white apple blossom, and yellow forsythia, showing how the use of white helps unify two colors that do not normally look good together—pink and yellow.

VAN GOGH'S SPECIAL COLOR COMBINATIONS can be displayed using cut flowers but also work with potted plants—with the obvious advantage that potted plants last considerably longer than cut flowers. Yellow daffodils and blue hyacinths are bulbs that can be forced for winter or early spring color to produce the yellow and blue combination that is considered the colors of Easter. Orange tulips and violet blue snow irises will also produce the orange and violet harmony he liked. Pots of black violas and white daisy chrysanthemums will produce the evocative black and white color contrast, but the best combination of all, and the most festive, is red and green. This makes a beautiful partnership for any time of year but is especially effective at Christmas, when red berries and evergreen boughs are readily available for decoration.

LEFT
Vase with Poppies, Cornflowers, Peonies, and Chrysanthemums *(1887) was the inspiration for this arrangement of common garden flowers, picked fresh. Van Gogh's original painting was an exercise in what he called painting "brutal extremes" after seeing the effect of bright colors in Impressionist paintings by Monet, Manet, and Renoir.*

OPPOSITE
Vincent van Gogh, Flowers in Blue Vase, *1887. Kröller-Müller Museum, Otterlo, Netherlands.*

Even with the availability of Oasis, many floral arrangers today prefer that flowers find their own natural placement within a vase, as van Gogh's did. Of all the containers van Gogh used, his personal favorite was one with a bulbous body and narrow neck, which he used repeatedly to arrange heavy flowers like crown imperials, sunflowers, irises, and roses. This particular shape allows flower stems to rest firmly against the inside belly of the vase, with the stems crisscrossed at the narrow neck to provide stability when fanned out evenly beyond the rim of the container.

In the florist's world, "main" material refers to the principal component of an arrangement. Even when you have an equal number of flowers available, it is better to allow one particular flower type or color to dominate. The main material is generally placed in position first, and then consideration is given to using "accent" material. Usually this is a flower that complements the main in some way—by introducing either a contrasting color or an analogous color. "Fill" is the third and final element, many times consisting of airy white flowers to make the arrangement sparkle and sometimes even black flowers to tone down a garish color like orange or yellow. Fill can also be grasses, twigs, and leaves (such as ferns) that introduce textural and structural qualities as well as color complements.

Even van Gogh's arrangements that appear to use flowers of one color (such as his blue irises) often show an accent of white or red to enrich the effect. In his more complex arrangements (such as *Vase with Poppies, Daisies, Cornflowers, and Peonies,* 1886) he was fastidious about the use of fill, sometimes even introducing a discordant color—like splashes of yellow in an arrangement of mostly pastel colors—to enliven the main and accent elements.

His preoccupation with floral arrangements is succinctly summed up in a letter to Theo: "What Pissarro says is true, you must boldly exaggerate the effects of either harmony or discord that colors produce."

favorite PLANTS

*"The cypresses are always occupying my thoughts.
I should like to make something of them like the canvases
of sunflowers, because it astonishes me that they have not
yet been done as I see them. And the green has a quality of
such distinction. It is a splash of black in a sunny landscape,
but it is one of the most interesting black notes, and the
most difficult to hit off exactly that I can imagine."*

<small>LETTER TO THEO (SUMMER 1889)</small>

Many of the Impressionists loved
bearded irises. Monet collected
them and van Gogh painted them
both in still life arrangements
and in the garden of the Asylum
of Saint-Paul. This bed of pale
blue irises is part of a wide border
that extends more than eighty feet
in Renoir's garden, contrasting
blue petals and blue-green spiky
foliage with the wall of a farmhouse where his gardener lived.

European olive trees estimated to be five hundred years old reflect the early morning light in Renoir's garden, near Nice. Both Renoir and van Gogh admired these trees for their strong sculptural qualities and near-human characteristics.

Vincent van Gogh, Olive Trees, *detail.*

VAN GOGH PRODUCED more than 2,100 drawings and paintings during the ten-year period of his career, an incredible output of work; and he painted flowers and gardens more than any other motif. Generally, he had very definite reasons for painting a particular plant, whether it was a flower, a tree, or a pot of chives on a windowsill, and we are fortunate to have detailed letters explaining his thinking. The cypresses of Provence, for example, made exclamation points in the landscape. They have a spirelike habit and black-green tones that provided the contrast he wanted for citron yellow sunsets and orange wheat fields ready for harvest.

Comparing van Gogh's likes among cultivated plants reveals how much they parallel those of other great Impressionist painters. Renoir wrote admiringly of the cypress in a similar vein to van Gogh's, and painted a grand old specimen in a churchyard across the way from his garden near Nice. Preferences among the Impressionists also included poppies and daisies, sunflowers and peonies, geraniums and roses—all commonly grown in parks and home gardens of the period. Among larger plants, they admired the chestnut for its huge clusters of white and pink blossoms, poplars for their pencil-straight trunks, olive trees for their tortuous outlines and silver leaves, and lilacs for their billowing clouds of fragrant flower clusters. Nothing exotic, but mostly common plants easily encountered during a walk along a country road. Though van Gogh shared the Impressionists' enthusiasm for these same commonplace plants, his flower portraits extend to a much wider range than any of the other painters to include bell-shaped crown imperials, spiky thistles, hooded arums, bristly wayside grasses, and tubular tuberoses—plants with more interesting flower shapes, petal colors, or leaf forms than the usual Impressionist plant palette.

The following descriptions highlight plants that van Gogh especially admired, together with some useful tips, cultural instructions, and planting suggestions.

ARUMS

According to art historian Stefan Zweig: "In the garden at Arles and the asylum, Van Gogh painted at the same speed, with the same ecstatic obsession with light, and with the same manic creative plentitude. Scarcely had he painted one of his white-hot canvases but his unerring brush was at work on the next."

We tend to think of van Gogh's gardens as sunlit places, vibrant with bright colors, and certainly no garden could be more colorful or white hot than his flower garden series in Arles, gleaming with marigolds and zinnias, and his rendering of a lilac garden within the walls of the asylum. But gardens are not all shimmering annuals and perennials drenched in sunlight, and when van Gogh was experiencing his worst bouts of depression, he sought dark, sinister motifs in eerie, shady places. Moreover, he was aware that his paintings were often a reflection of his mood swings, noting that a series of landscapes under troubled skies were metaphors for his troubled mind. His most severe bouts of melancholy occurred during his stay at the Asylum of Saint-Paul, and though many of the paintings of the garden pulsate with white-hot colors, many communicate foreboding, gloom, and

nial, is not really a lily but a member of a large plant family that includes calla lilies and jack-in-the-pulpits. The arum is shade tolerant, and the curious hooded spathe half encloses a pokerlike protrusion called a spadix. The flower hoods appear in early spring among clumps of erect, arrow-shaped dark green leaves, which

Sinister-looking Italian arums have arrow-shaped leaves and strange greenish white hoods surrounding a powdery yellow spadix. They grow wild in the woodland at the Asylum of Saint-Paul, and van Gogh painted them during periods of melancholy.

death. Indeed, during a period of suicidal tendencies, the asylum's garden took on the aspect of a garden of evil—reflected in van Gogh's images of tortuous trunks of oak trees suffocating with ivy, ugly black beetles feasting on funereal white roses, and dark, towering pines striking the sky like venomous snakes. But the most sinister image of all is of a death's-head moth on a group of ghostlike hooded arum lilies, their poisonous, blood red berry clusters visible in the background like the bloodshot eyes of a vampire.

The Italian arum lily *(Arum italicum),* a hardy peren-

can be exotically marbled. After the spathe dies, the leaves generally die down during the heat of summer, leaving a decorative stalk topped by clusters of bright red berries.

The Italian arum is tolerant of boggy soils, and we use it in the shade of river birches in company with white, pink, and maroon hellebores, another shade-loving plant that van Gogh admired and painted. The hellebore known as Lenten rose *(Helleborus orientalis)* has evergreen leaves that resemble pachysandra and nodding cup-shaped flowers that flower early with the arums. Both are widely adapted, thriving in zones 5 to 9.

CHESTNUTS

Van Gogh painted the chestnut tree in many forms—as an avenue in *Chestnut Trees in Blossom* (1890), twice as lone sentinels in *Chestnut Tree in Blossom* (1887 and 1890), as a flowering extravaganza in *Couples in the Voyer d'Argenson Park* (1887), and their flower clusters in close up (*Blossoming Chestnut Branches,* 1890).

The chestnut most often featured in van Gogh's paintings is the hardy European horse chestnut or white buckeye (*Aesculus hippocastanum*), flowering mostly in white. While the common chestnut is a tall, billowing tree unsuitable for small gardens, there is a hardy red-flowering species from North America (*Aesculus pavia*) called the red buckeye, which is much smaller and more practical for garden culture. The European and American species have been crossed to make a hybrid, *A. x carnea,* which has the most extensive color range of all, including yellow, orange, red, pink, apricot, and white, and these appear to be the featured trees in van Gogh's painting of the Voyer d'Argenson Park. The white European buckeye is the hardiest (zones 3–8), while the red buckeye is only slightly less hardy (zones 5–8).

CROWN IMPERIALS

Van Gogh's painting of a copper vase of crown imperials is well known. Much less familiar is a mass planting he painted in a garden setting, since its whereabouts is now unknown.

The crown imperial is available in basically two colors—orange and yellow. It grows from a doughnut-shaped bulb that is susceptible to rot in moist or heavy clay soils. Slender flower stems of glossy green with spear-shaped leaves are topped by a cluster of bell-shaped flowers beneath a rakish crown of spiky leaves like a pineapple's.

All parts of a crown imperial have a musky odor, which is not objectionable outdoors but becomes unpleasant when the leaves or stems are bruised and confined to a room. Planting of the bulbs should be done in fall, in full sun or light shade. The bells are extremely attractive when viewed against a blue sky or seen against carpets of blue Siberian squill and grape hyacinths. The plants are hardy and will overwinter in northern gardens if the soil is sandy or gravelly to provide sharp drainage. The ideal growing range of hardiness for crown imperials is amazing for a hardy bulb, extending across zones 5 to 9.

Chestnuts have generous flower clusters called candles, usually white or pink in color, and van Gogh painted them often. They are a popular street tree in Paris and Provence. This specimen is a hybrid, Aesculus x carnea, *a cross between a European and an American chestnut.*

ABOVE RIGHT

Crown imperials have an arrangement of leaves and flowers that van Gogh greatly admired. The orange flowers are shaped like bells, hanging down in clusters, with a rakish arrangement of leaves on top of the flower cluster, as on a pineapple. They are especially beautiful in the company of blue flowers like the grape hyacinths and violas shown here—indeed, van Gogh recommended orange and blue as good companions for his sister to try in her garden.

Vincent van Gogh,
Fritillaries in a
Copper Vase, *1886.*
Musée d'Orsay, Paris.

CYPRESSES AND CEDARS

The evergreen cypresses of Provence (*Juniperus communis*) are not true cypresses but junipers. In both habit and color they are similar to the red cedar of North America (*Juniperus virginiana*), which also is not really a cedar but also a juniper. In Asia there is another look-alike juniper—*Juniperus chinensis.* Today much hybridizing has been done to produce varieties that are considered to be more attractive than the wild species (including some wonderful blue kinds), but it must be remembered that it was the black-green coloration that van Gogh especially liked. Varieties that produce the same effect include the Chinese juniper 'Obelisk' and the upright Lawson cypress, *Chamaecyparisus lawsoniana* 'Columnaris'. The Lawson cypress is one of the most widely adapted upright evergreens, extending across zones 5 to 9.

The "blue cedar" that van Gogh admired so much in *The Garden of the Poets* is undoubtedly the blue Atlas cedar, *Cedrus atlantica*—perhaps the variety 'Glauca', remarkable for its deep blue coloration and the way it sweeps its lower branches sideways to cover large areas of lawn. The Atlas cedar thrives in zones 6 to 9.

DAHLIAS

Neither the dwarf bedding–type dahlias grown from seed or the giant dinner-plate dahlias grown from tubers are the kind that van Gogh painted so frequently in arrangements and cottage gardens. Rather, the medium-size decorative dahlias grown mostly from tubers were the subject of his work. He obviously liked the dahlia for its impressive color range, especially its rich reds and yellows, for few common flowers can match the iridescence and perfect symmetry of a dahlia blossom.

In his painting *Memory of the Garden at Etten* (1888), he used yellow dahlias as a bold contrast to dark background elements, showing them massed in a bed to themselves. In his painting of a cottage garden near Arles, he expressed pleasure at having tall, dusky, maroon-colored dahlias to contrast with the golden blossoms of marigolds.

Dahlias can be tender annuals or tender perennials, depending on variety. Flowering from midsummer to fall frost, they have mostly daisy-shaped blooms that demand full sun and a fertile soil with good drainage. The hollow stems are brittle, and so the tall kinds should be staked to provide strong support.

We like to mix dahlias and gladiolus together, for they have a similar wide color range and bloom at the same time, in midsummer. The spires of gladiolus flowers reach up among the dahlias to create a beautiful hot color combination. Dahlias grown as annuals are suitable for all zones. The tubers will overwinter from zones 8 south.

DAISIES—MARGUERITE AND OX-EYE

Many of van Gogh's still life arrangements feature daisies, and they are prominent in several of his garden landscapes, featured as shimmering sweeps of white in company with lilac bushes, irises, buttercups, and poppies. In addition to the hardy ox-eye daisy *(Chrysanthemum leucanthemum)*, he painted the more tender Marguerite daisy *(C. frutescens)*, both of which prefer full sun for spring flowering.

Ox-eye and Marguerite daisies should not be confused with the larger-flowered Shasta daisy—a hardy hybrid known as *Chrysanthemum x superbum,* which is summer-flowering and not as hardy or long-lived as a perennial.

We use masses of ox-eye daisies in mixed perennial borders, where the white petals help to brighten the solid colors of peonies, bearded irises, and Oriental poppies, and also as components of wildflower mixtures. The hardiness range of ox-eye daisies is zones 3 to 8; of Marguerites, zones 8 south.

LEFT

Vincent van Gogh, Flowers in Blue Vase, *detail.*

RIGHT

Ox-eye daisies in company with blue Siberian irises. Van Gogh especially liked to see great sweeps of daisies, irises, and buttercups mingling their blossoms in the meadows around Arles.

Foxgloves in a Mediterranean-style garden. Van Gogh used the foxglove in a portrait of his physician, Dr. Gachet, to signify his profession, since the doctor used digitalis—a drug derived from the plant—in his treatment of mental disorders.

FOXGLOVES

Van Gogh rendered two paintings of the sad, widowed Dr. Paul Gachet, dressed in a yachting cap and jacket, "with the heartbroken expression of our time," according to a letter he wrote to Gauguin. The doctor is holding a spray of purple foxgloves, no doubt gathered from his garden, symbolizing his profession as a physician. Foxgloves are a source of digitalis, a poison that can be used in controlled doses to treat heart ailments and mental stress. They are also beautiful garden plants, creating spires of bell-shaped spotted flowers in mostly red, pink, purple, white, and yellow. Though there is an annual variety, 'Foxy', which will flower the first year from seed, the taller varieties are biennials that create a rosette of velvetlike leaves the first season and then flower the following spring. After flowering they set prodigious quantities of seed and will self-sow into bare soil in sun or shade.

We like to use foxgloves extensively to create a red-pink-silver color combination, especially in lightly shaded areas, and tall lamb's ears for silvery tones. Foxgloves' range of hardiness extends from zones 4 to 8.

GERANIUMS

In recent times geraniums have often been given a bad rap—too commonplace is the general thinking. But they were commonplace in van Gogh's day too, and he loved them no less because they produce one of the most beautiful color harmonies in all of nature—a bold splash of vibrant red against vigorous green leaves.

As we've discussed, red and green are opposites on the color wheel, and when you put opposites together, the effect is to intensify each color. In other words, the red petals appear redder and the green leaves appear greener. Monet felt the same way about geraniums and planted them in island beds within view of the porch of his pink house, interplanted

geraniums are used as annuals for summer flowering, they are suitable for all hardiness zones.

GRASSES

Van Gogh liked to use grasses in many forms—painting close-ups of clump-forming blue sedge grasses spangled with wildflowers; incorporating orange marsh grasses and wheat as broad brushstrokes to color a landscape; even rendering the queen of grasses—bamboo—in a painting he made of a Japanese landscape. With their slender, shimmering, arching leaf blades, grasses can be used in a multitude of ways to glorify a garden—either by themselves as a grass garden, mixed into perennial borders to soften the stiffness associated with most other flowering perennials, or as components of a tapestry garden to provide wispy, textural contrasts.

Not everyone has the space to reproduce some of van Gogh's golden wheat fields, but smaller-scale wheat field effects can be made using any number of ornamental grasses, especially varieties of maiden grass (*Miscanthus species*) and fountain grass (*Pennisetum species*). These turn shades of amber in autumn and sprout shimmering flower plumes of silver, red, and black, depending on variety.

Most grasses are associated with open meadows, and while it is true that the majority prefer sunny, well-drained sites, many will tolerate shade and moist soils. Though the predominant color in summer is green, the color range can include yellow ('Bowles Golden' grass), blue ('Elijah Blue' fescue), and even red ('Red Baron' bloodgrass), so that a landscape can be "painted" in grasses, like the van Gogh composition of fishermen's cottages among orange and blue sedge grasses in the Camargue.

Grasses are among the most widely adapted of all plants, ranging from the Antarctic to the Arctic Circle, and varieties such as *Miscanthus sinensis* have a wide hardiness range, extending from zones 4 to 9.

Ivy-leaf geraniums and Boston ivy decorate a French courtyard, showing how well red and pink flowers are complemented by green. Van Gogh also suggested combining geraniums and poppies in red tones for a powerful red and green color harmony.

OPPOSITE

Van Gogh had begun painting grasses in the countryside around Paris and continued to do so in Provence, especially at the Asylum of Saint-Paul. This grass garden is seen in autumn, when the leaf blades turn shades of amber.

with standard tree-form pink roses. I have discovered that geraniums look sensational in terra-cotta pots placed against rough stonework, such as a flight of stone steps. Two kinds of geraniums can look wonderful together—the common bedding geranium (*Pelargonium x hortorum*) and the less familiar ivy-leaf geranium (*Pelargonium peltatum*), which has a similar color range—red, pink, white, and orange. Bedding geraniums are best for pots, while ivy-leafs are sensational used in windowbox planters and large urns so their cascading stems can drape like a curtain.

Both kinds of geraniums are ever-blooming, and so a long-lasting display can be enjoyed from spring all through summer and right up to fall frosts. Since

HOLLYHOCKS

Van Gogh painted hollyhocks in arrangements and referred to them fondly in letters. These impressive spirelike flowering plants can take color high into the sky and help to fill the void between low plantings and the leaf canopy. There are basically two kinds of hollyhocks—the single-flowered with cup-shaped blooms and the double-flowered with pom-pom blooms. Mixtures of both are available in a wide range of colors, including red, pink, yellow, orange, apricot, and white. There are also several shades of maroon that extend to black, and these can look exquisite growing among orange, yellow, or white flowers. We like to use hollyhocks to tower above picket fences, and plant the black in company with white summer phlox, yellow sunflowers, and blue larkspur. Hollyhocks are suitable for zones 3 to 9.

IRISES

The iris family is extremely large and the most diverse in color after orchids, to which they are distantly related. Their color range includes the entire color spectrum—red, blue, yellow, orange, violet, and green. There are even brown and black irises, plus numerous bicolors and tricolors. Van Gogh's favorite iris was the bearded iris (*I. x germanica*), especially blue, but he also painted white, red, yellow, and black varieties.

The bearded iris is hardy and grows over a wide climatic range. The flowers have a pleasant peppery fragrance, though each flower lasts only one day. However, since each flower stem often carries a dozen or more buds, a flowering period of up to two weeks can be expected—longer if early and late-season varieties are used in a planting so that blooming is staggered. Some bearded irises are also repeat-flowering, producing a second flush of bloom in autumn. They are easily propagated by dividing the tuberous roots (called rhizomes) after flowering in spring. These divisions grow plants identical to the parent.

The flower form of a bearded iris is unique, composed of a set of upward-arching petals called standards and a set of downward, broader petals called falls. Sometimes the standards and falls are different colors, one of the colors being white. This flash of

Van Gogh discovered the allure of bearded irises in the Asylum of Saint-Paul, where he painted mostly blue, black, and white tones. Since the color range of bearded irises is one of the most diverse in the plant kingdom, a special iris garden like this can sport a broad spectrum of colors.

The color harmony of blue and yellow is easily achieved with bearded irises, since blue and yellow are the predominant colors. This planting shows a newer blue hybrid in company with an old yellow and purple bicolor variety, 'Gracchus'.

white is highly desirable because it helps to brighten the other color, usually blue or yellow.

Van Gogh painted bearded irises both as indoor floral arrangements and in garden settings, including violet blues partnered with orange calendulas. This is how we like to grow them, massed in a bed to themselves and underplanted with yellow pansies or orange calendulas. There are several varieties of black iris, and these we partner with ox-eye daisies to produce a startling black and white combination like the black irises and white daisies seen in van Gogh's painting *Lilacs* (1889), showing a corner of the asylum garden at Saint-Rémy. In the same painting he partners black irises with what appear to be yellow buttercups. Bearded irises are also good companions for pink and red peonies, red Oriental poppies, and pink dame's rocket.

Ideally, the tubers should be planted in a sunny, well-drained position, with their tops exposed above the soil, since they like to bake in the sun. Bearded irises are widely adapted, suitable for zones 3 to 9. Other types of iris, especially European flag irises (*I. pseudacorus*) and Japanese water irises (*Iris ensata*), prefer moist soils, even soil permanently covered by shallow water.

IVY—ENGLISH

Most people are familiar with van Gogh's stupendously colorful cottage garden paintings with their blaze of oranges and reds, notably *Flowering Garden with Path* (1888), but when his brother opened a box of paintings van Gogh sent him from the Asylum of Saint-Paul, he expressed keen pleasure at the sight of a woodland with an undergrowth of ivy, the ivy creeping up the trunks right into the leaf canopy. There is nothing quite like common English ivy to create a sinister atmosphere or suggest a garden of great age, and I know of no plants that take deep shade as successfully as English ivy. The small-leaf variety known as 'Needlepoint' is particularly appealing because it is not as coarse as regular English ivy, and for a lighter effect I also use variegated forms, such as 'Little Diamond' (mottled green leaves edged in white) and 'Gold Heart' (yellow leaves edged in green). Excellent companions to ivy in shade gardens are ferns (especially the ostrich fern) and hostas (especially blue forms like 'Blue Angel' and yellow and blue variegated forms like 'Frances Williams'). Most English ivies are widely adapted, suitable for zones 5 to 10.

Ivy and moss cloak a tree in the garden of Le Vasterival, on the Normandy coast. Van Gogh expressed his liking for stones and trees with a patina of algae, moss, or ivy in a letter he wrote from Saint-Rémy to his mother: "Here one never sees those moss-covered roofs on the barns or cottages as at home."

LAVENDER

In the mountains of Provence, lavender can be found growing wild. Van Gogh painted an entire field with the uniform rows presenting long lines of perspective, leading the eye to the village of Saintes-Maries-de-la-Mer in the Camargue. There are several kinds grown in gardens—English lavender (*Lavandula angustifolia*), French lavender (*L. stoechas*), and the lavender of Provence (*L. x intermedia* 'Grosso'), which is a hybrid between English and Portuguese. English lavender and the lavender of Provence look alike, though English lavender is hardier and the kind that should be used in northern gardens. Many people have a problem growing lavender because it is subject to rotting in heavy clay or moist soils. For a beautiful display of lavender, it is worth creating a special bed incorporating gravel to provide the sharp drainage lavender needs.

Hardy varieties of English lavender such as 'Hidcote' (deep blue) and 'Munstead' (powder blue), are suitable for zones 5 to 8. Tender lavenders, such as French lavender, are suitable for zones 8 south.

LILACS

The French have always been famous for their lilac displays in gardens and public parks, and today the most desirable varieties are a strain known as French hybrids, developed from the common lilac and producing extra-large flower clusters. Van Gogh painted common lilacs as flowering shrubs in the garden of the Asylum of Saint-Paul and as a bouquet of several colors. Flowering in spring, lilacs range in color from purple, pink, and red to powder blue, white, and pale yellow. In his painting *Lilacs* (1889), they are flowering in the asylum garden in company with white and yellow daisies, yellow buttercups, and black irises.

At our farm we have several large specimens of common lilac that are at least forty years old, under-

Pronounced lines of perspective are produced by rows of lavender near the Asylum of Saint-Paul, in a pattern like that seen in van Gogh's painting entitled View of Saintes-Maries (1888).

planted mostly with drifts of irises, peonies, and Oriental poppies. We also have younger specimens of the French hybrids in an extensive color range, planted in semicircles to create a flowery bower and a sheltered place for a slatted bench. Lilacs are highly fragrant and make beautiful floral arrangements. The French hybrids are ideal for northern gardens (zones 4 to 8); a California strain known as the Descanso performs better in southern gardens.

A slatted bench is placed near a mature lilac bush so the fragrance of the blossoms can be appreciated in early spring. Van Gogh painted mature plants like this in the Asylum of Saint-Paul and cut stems for a still life arrangement.

RIGHT
Vincent van Gogh, Lilac Bush, 1889. Hermitage, St. Petersburg.

MARIGOLDS

In his correspondence van Gogh referred to marigolds as "Africans" because the common name for the tall kind is African marigold. (The small ones are referred to as French marigolds.) Both are misnomers, as the marigold is native only to Central America.

In today's gardens the marigold is commonplace, and people tend to like them or despise them—probably because they are so assertive in the garden and some people find the odor of the stems and leaves unpleasant.

However, when you take a careful look at van Gogh's *Flower Garden* series, painted at Arles in the summer of 1888, you will see that the garden would not be so beautiful without its brilliant splashes of yellow and orange from masses of African marigolds.

We find African marigolds and dahlia-flowered zinnias good companions, and we use them for dramatic color impact in our cutting garden. As one visitor exclaimed when he saw the mass of cheerful yellow and orange marigolds, "They seem to grab all the sunlight and hand it right back to you."

Since marigolds and zinnias are quick-growing annuals, they are suitable for all zones.

OLEANDERS

The oleander is a flowering shrub that is prolific throughout the Mediterreanean. It can be grown outdoors in frost-free areas like southern California and Florida, where it is frequently used as a flowering hedge. In northern gardens it is easy to grow in a roomy container such as a Versailles planter and will flower continuously outdoors all summer. Then it can be taken indoors when frost threatens in autumn. Plants prefer full sun and are drought and heat resistant. The pink makes an especially beautiful tree accent for a deck or patio.

We like to grow pink oleanders in tubs so the flowering canopy reaches up to the blue flowers of clematis for a strong pink and blue color contrast. A word of caution, however—all parts of an oleander are poisonous, including the leaves, flowers, roots, and branches. Outdoors the oleander thrives in zones 8 south.

169

OLIVE TREES

Van Gogh held the European olive (*Olea europa*) in such high esteem that he flew into a rage when he saw how unfeelingly his artist friends Gauguin and Bernard both portrayed the olive in religious works showing Christ in the Garden of Olives. Gauguin even had the audacity to portray himself as Christ, a point that may have contributed to van Gogh's outrage.

In his desire to show the olive as he saw it, van Gogh worked relentlessly night and day in an olive orchard just beyond the walls of the Asylum of Saint-Paul, expressing his pleasure at the olive's silvery leaves and twisting branches and its ability to change colors according to the play of light and season of the year.

Unfortunately, the European olive—which lives to a great age and matures into a gnarled, twisted shape with a splayed base—is too tender for northern gardens, but some of its hardier relatives, notably the Russian olive (*Elaeagnus angustifolia*), can make a good substitute. Though not an orchard tree, the Russian olive displays similar silvery leaves and contorted branches. While the European olive will thrive in zones 8 south, the Russian olive has a hardiness range from zones 3 to 8.

The cloudlike effect of peach trees in bloom shows the challenge van Gogh found in capturing their vibrant beauty when the orchards around Arles began to flower in early spring.

OPPOSITE

This garden space combines several elements gleaned from studying the garden philosophy of van Gogh: billowing flowering shrubs; decorative bark and strong structural elements.

PEACHES AND OTHER FLOWERING TREES

The fruiting peach trees that van Gogh painted near Arles can be difficult to grow because they are susceptible to insects and diseases. Since it was the flowering effect van Gogh most admired, it is best to consider using other trees with masses of glittering blossoms to produce what van Gogh described as "astounding gaiety." I have re-created the flowering extravaganza of his orchard series by using mostly rose-pink Eastern redbud trees *(Cercis canadensis)* and disease-resistant varieties of pink-flowering crab apples *(Malus x hybrida),* underplanted with a profuse-flowering evergreen azalea, *Rhododendron poukhanense* (aka *R. yedoense).* They all bloom together at the same time in early spring. Viewed against a blue sky, these trees and shrubs make a spectacular pink and blue color harmony.

The true peach *(Prunus persica)* is hardy from zones 6 to 9; the Eastern redbud extends into zone 5, while many crab apple hybrids will grow in zone 3. *Rhododendron poukhanense* is remarkable for its hardiness range—zones 5 to 9.

PINES

Cedars, junipers, and pines are all evergreen conifers that van Gogh admired and painted—cedars for their broad, blue sweeping branches; junipers for their obelisk forms in the gardens and landscapes of Provence; and pines for their ability to create tall, sinuous trunks with topknots of green foliage.

The pines he admired and painted in the asylum garden at Saint-Rémy have beautiful orange-brown fissured bark and are commonly called umbrella pines (*Pinus pinea*) for their lovely dome-shaped skyline silhouette. But they are tender plants, and for northern climates a better choice would be the hardy Scotch pine (*P. sylvestris*) or the Austrian pine (*P. nigra*), both of which display handsome bark coloration similar to that of the Mediterranean umbrella pine.

Van Gogh cherished pines not only for their ornamental bark and bold skyline shape but also for the rich brown carpet of fallen needles used as mulch along woodland paths.

We have a large grove of young Scotch pines that one day I hope to see pencil the skyline with their distinctive rakish silhouettes, but in the meantime they are an endless source of decorative organic mulch and resin-rich kindling for fires and barbecues. Hardiness among pines depends on variety. The tender Mediterranean umbrella pine is best for zones 8 south, while the Scotch pine extends from zones 3 to 7.

POPPIES

Van Gogh painted poppies in every conceivable way—fields of poppies, gardens planted with poppies, and arrangements of poppies. These were all annual corn poppies, usually depicted against green backgrounds to gain the red and green contrast he so much admired.

Corn poppies are best grown from seed sown directly into the garden because they grow quickly and will not tolerate any root disturbance, such as transplanting. Choose either Shirley poppy (*Papaver*

rhoeas), which is available in a mixture of mostly pinks and reds, or the Flanders' field poppy (*P. commutatum*), which is scarlet red. The variety 'Ladybird' has beautiful black petal markings.

To get annual poppies blooming early in the spring, it is best to sow the seed in the late summer or early fall in full sun. This allows the plants to form a crown of green leaves that will survive even harsh winters and bloom extra early in spring. A succession of bloom is possible by sowing again in early spring for midsummer bloom, and in late spring for fall bloom. The seed is tiny and merely requires soil contact in order to germinate, though raking the seed into the upper soil surface is beneficial.

Red poppies and blue cornflowers can look wonderful planted together in a wildflower meadow. In addition to the annual kinds, we use the perennial Oriental poppy in perennial borders, in company with blue bearded irises and pink peonies. Since corn and Shirley poppies are fast-growing annuals, they are suitable for all zones. Though poppies are not long-lived in arrangements, the cut flower life can be extended by plunging the stems up to their necks in water and, immediately before arranging, searing the base of the stem to seal the moisture in.

ROSES

The roses van Gogh said he admired in Provence were large flamboyant red roses—probably hybrids of *Rosa gallica,* which are used prolifically in home gardens, their long canes often splayed out against beige walls. But he more often painted shrub roses with more diminutive flowers, their avalanche of blossoms billowing and spilling into pathways. Recognizable roses in his paintings are a pink single-flowered variety named "Complicata" and pink "Maiden's Blush"—both old garden roses.

A *field of annual poppies near the Asylum of Saint-Paul, where van Gogh admitted himself to be treated for mental problems. Poppies were a favorite subject of the painter—both in arrangements and in the landscape. He encountered them not only in Provence but also at Auvers, north of Paris, where he lived his final days.*

Two vigorous, extra-hardy shrub roses that always provide a wonderful display and survive the depredations of both pests and diseases are 'Meidiland Red' and pink 'Bonica', both of which are ever-blooming from June until fall frosts. We partner 'Red Meidiland' with silvery lamb's ears to generate the red and silver motif that van Gogh painted using red poppies and lavender foliage. Since roses are widely distributed throughout the world, there are varieties suitable for all zones.

SUNFLOWERS

Sunflowers and lavender are synonymous with Provence, the two often growing together in adjacent fields for oil production—sunflower oil for use in cooking and lavender for use in cosmetics and perfumes. Van Gogh painted both the single-flowered sunflower with a starburst of petals and the double-flowered kind with multiple rows of petals forming an almost ball-shaped flower head. Though his paintings showing arrangements of sunflowers are his most famous, when he lived in Montmartre he also painted them in gardens and as seed heads.

One of the best double forms of sunflower is 'Teddy Bear', which is golden yellow. It forms a bushy plant about four feet high and blooms continuously from midsummer to fall frost. Plants grow quickly from seed sown directly into the garden in full sun.

Mixtures of multicolored sunflowers are available today. These not only display yellow flowers but also orange, white, lemon, and maroon—some with contrasting dark zones and black centers. 'Autumn Beauty' is an especially good mixture. The more these are cut, the more new flower stems appear.

Yellow sunflowers and the blue morning glory 'Heavenly Blue' look spectacular together. Since sunflowers are fast-growing annuals, they are suitable for all zones.

THISTLES

With their reputation as wayside weeds, thistles may seem like an odd plant to be attracted to, but van Gogh painted them both in an arrangement and outdoors, obviously liking their bold sculptural beauty. The thistle he usually encountered in Provence was the milk thistle *(Silybum marianum),* which has beautiful broad, spiky leaves marbled white and dark green. In frost-free areas like California, they are considered noxious weeds, and so a more appropriate plant for gardens is the Scotch thistle *(Onopordum acanthium),* a biennial plant growing to nine feet high and displaying large, silvery, sharply indented leaves. Small purple flowers crown the plants in the summer of the second season.

The Scotch thistle can create a bold architectural accent in a perennial border, especially in contrast to swaying ornamental grasses and stiff red-hot poker plants. The milk thistle is best for zones 8 south if flowering is desired, though it can be grown for foliage effect only. The Scotch thistle is suitable for zones 6 to 9 for flowering effect, farther north still for only foliage effect where winters are severe.

YUCCA

Although associated with southern gardens, hardy species of yucca exist—notably *Yucca filamentosa* (Spanish dagger) and *Yucca glauca* (soapweed). Van Gogh painted them prominently in cottage gardens of the Camargue and also in Dr. Gachet's garden at Auvers-sur-Oise, north of Paris. He admired them for their stiff, spiky leaves and the contrast they offer with softer foliage plants like geraniums.

Yuccas are evergreen and will bloom in early summer, sending up a tall flower stem resembling a gigantic asparagus spear, which opens out into a candelabra of gleaming white bell-shaped flowers. They are highly drought tolerant and require full sun and well-drained soil. Spanish dagger thrives outdoors from zone 5 south; soapweed from zone 6 south.

CONCLUSION

"But for one's health, as you say, it is very necessary to work in the garden and to see the flowers growing."

LETTER FROM VAN GOGH TO HIS MOTHER, SHORTLY BEFORE HIS SUICIDE (SUMMER 1890)

A *section of van Gogh's Walk at Saint-Rémy, Provence, so called because it encircles the walls of the asylum and leads to many of the landscapes he painted. This section shows redbud trees in bloom along the stout stone wall provided for the safety and privacy of the mental patients.*

THE IMPRESSIONIST MASTERS were absorbed with plants and flowers, and many of them were able to create marvelous gardens. Monet's garden near Paris, Cézanne's garden at Aix-en-Provence, and Renoir's garden near Nice survive to this day, mostly as a result of American funding. The gardens of Pissarro, Manet, and Caillebotte, unfortunately, no longer exist. Van Gogh briefly cultivated a garden in London, where he worked for several years as a teacher and art

dealer, and he helped tend his father's parsonage garden at Nuenan when he lived with his parents. But his perpetual poverty and erratic mental condition prevented his having a home and garden of his own.

It's interesting to speculate about what kind of garden van Gogh might have had if he had survived into old age and had gone on to receive artistic acclaim. Would it have been a sinister garden like Cézanne's at Aix-en-Provence, with its emphasis on eerie paths leading through shrubbery to create leafy tunnels? Or would it have been more like Renoir's garden near Nice, with its five-hundred-year-old olive orchard and sunny wildflower meadows? Or like Monet's garden at Giverny, north of Paris, which actually consisted of three independent gardens—a flower garden for cutting, a vegetable garden for food production, and a water garden for introspection?

It's conceivable that van Gogh's garden would have included elements of all three—the color harmonies that Monet used (but not with such a controlling hand), the pantiled old farmhouse that Renoir saved from destruction and used as a landscape accent (but probably with a thatch roof), and paths creating leaf tunnels like those in Cézanne's garden, with coiling trunks striking the sky to make a cathedral of greenery.

If he had chosen to settle in the South, he would certainly have wanted olive trees like those in Renoir's garden, for their animated growth gave van Gogh great pleasure in ways that Renoir similarly expressed. If he had lived in the North, he might have substituted oak or English walnut for their ability to produce the gnarled, contorted character of ancient olive trees. He probably would have integrated flowers and vegetables, as his old friend Pissarro did—not necessarily mixing them for ornamental effect but contrasting them in separate plots, as in his painting *Memory of the Garden at Etten* (1888), in which beds of cabbages contrast with beds of annuals. Undoubtedly van Gogh would have planted his garden to paint, and like Monet, he might have considered it to be a great work of art!

Van Gogh gardens on canvas range from sunlit spaces bright with colorful annuals to shady corners verdant with bold, comforting foliage effects. He was dogmatic, highly opinionated, intelligent, and above all, an incredibly keen observer of nature. A look at his gardens and landscapes reveals planting ideas that are different from those of traditional gardens—bold

Tool shed planted to resemble cottages painted by van Gogh in Auvers, the Camargue, and Holland.

ideas hit you like a thunderbolt. Surely we need more thunderbolts in gardens.

Van Gogh had no doubt that his work would eventually be appreciated. Even before he began painting, as a teacher in London, he felt he was destined to make a mark on the world. But toward the end of his life, in an analysis of his art, he speculated in a letter to Theo that someone even better than he might set the art world on fire: "You must feel as I do that such a one will come . . . But the painter of the future will be a colorist such as never yet existed . . . this painter who is to come—I can't imagine him living in cafés, working away with a lot of false teeth, and going to soldiers' brothels as I do . . ."

It has been more than a hundred years since van Gogh's premature death, and such an artist has yet to come. When you stand before his most powerful landscapes—those in the Van Gogh Museum in Amsterdam or the Kröller-Müller State Museum at Otterlo—the energy that seems to pulsate from massive seed heads of sunflowers or golden wheat fields against indigo skies glows like nothing else. And you cannot help but wonder—can it really get any better than this?

and definitive in scope, yet filled with important structure and detail, such as moss coating a roof, ivy cloaking a tree trunk, and lichens covering stonework. These ideas are not for the faint-hearted or chic. As garden writer Olive Dunn realized when she planted van Gogh's orange and black garden, these

chronology

1853 Born March 30 at Groot-Zundert, Holland. Named Vincent after an earlier child who died at birth.

1857 Birth of van Gogh's brother Theo. The two become close siblings and take an oath of life-long loyalty to each other.

1869 Employed at the Hague branch of his uncle's art dealership, Goupil & Company.

1873 Transferred to London branch of Goupil & Company. Planted a flower garden at rear of his lodgings in Richmond.

1875 Transferred to Paris branch of Goupil & Company.

1876 Dismissed from Goupil & Company.

1877 Worked in a bookshop at Dordrecht, Holland. Moved to Amsterdam.

1878 Became a preacher and missionary to an impoverished community of coal miners in the Borinage, Belgium.

1879 Dismissed from missionary duties for eccentric behavior.

1880 Took up painting. Enrolled in art classes in Brussels.

1881 Returned home to Etten to live with his parents. Began painting, mostly in somber colors, including images of his father's parsonage garden. Fell in love with his widowed cousin, Kee Vos, a relationship that generated parental disapproval and resulted in rejection.

1882 Moved to the Hague and shared his lodgings with a destitute pregnant prostitute, Sien Hoornik.

1883 Ended relationship with Sien and left the Hague for Drenthe, then to his parents' new home and garden in Nuenan.

1885 At Nuenan painted *The Potato Eaters*— a family of peasants enjoying a meal of potatoes dug fresh from the garden. "I have tried to emphasize that these people, eating their potatoes in the lamplight, have dug the earth with those very hands they put in the dish, and so it speaks of manual labor and how they have honestly earned their food."

1886 Enrolled in art classes in Antwerp, Belgium, but soon became disillusioned with his teachers. Left Antwerp for Paris to room with his brother Theo, who had established himself as an art dealer. Met the Impressionist painter Pissarro, fell under the spell of Impressionism, and declared himself an Impressionist. Also met Seurat and found his pointillist technique fascinating. To lighten his palette, threw himself into a frenzy of painting floral still life arrangements. Also painted several views of expansive vegetable gardens. Then wandered further afield to paint several public gardens, notably *People in the Park at Asnières* (1887), which uses elements of both Impressionism and pointillism to show the vibrancy of pink and white chestnut trees in bloom. Began collecting Japanese woodblock prints and arranged an exhibition of Japanese prints.

1888 With financial support from his brother, moved to the South of France seeking new challenges. Rented a house in Arles and seized on blooming fruit trees as a favorite motif, then numerous garden motifs. In summer, painted a series of sunflower arrangements and was joined by Gauguin. Suffered a mental seizure and cut off part of his ear following a violent argument with Gauguin, who left for Paris. Following hospital treatment in Arles, admitted himself to the nearby asylum at Saint-Rémy for continued treatment of his mental disorder.

1889 Mental seizures continued. Attempted suicide by swallowing his paints and the turpentine used to fill the hospital's lamps. While receiving treatment, spent a year painting in and around the walls of the asylum, notably images of the walled garden, olive orchards, and wildflower meadows. Received news that Theo had married and soon after learned that his wife, Johanna, was pregnant. Johanna wrote to van Gogh: "I am going to tell you a great piece of news, on which we have been concentrating a great deal of attention lately—it is that next winter, toward February probably, we hope to have a baby, a pretty baby boy—whom we are going to call Vincent, if you will kindly consent to be his godfather. Of course, I know we must not count on it too much, and that it may well be a little girl, but Theo and I cannot help imagining that the baby will be a boy— please write us your opinion of our little boy, as a boy it must be."

1890 Overjoyed at the birth of the baby Vincent. Moved to Auvers, north of Paris, under the care of Dr. Paul Gachet, but soon lost his faith in the doctor's ability to cure him. Harbored romantic feelings for the doctor's nineteen-year-old daughter, Marguerite, but Dr. Gachet disapproved. Theo's newborn son took ill and his medical needs strained the family's finances. Borrowed a pistol on the pretext of scaring crows in a wheat field he wished to paint. Botched a suicide attempt, staggered to the village for help with a bullet lodged near his stomach, and died two days later in Theo's care. (Theo himself died six months later. Both he and his brother were buried side by side in the churchyard at Auvers, in a small cemetery surrounded by wheat fields.)

places to visit

Because many places have opening dates and times that change with the seasons, check first before planning a visit.

France

VAN GOGH'S WALK, ARLES, PROVENCE

Starts at the place du Forum, where gift shops sell a booklet entitled Arles Van Gogh, *with maps that show the location of many of van Gogh's motifs, including the nearby hospital garden (now a crafts center) with its restored courtyard garden.*

VAN GOGH'S WALK, AUVERS-SUR-OISE, NEAR PARIS

At the tourist office in the Manoir des Colombiers, located at rue Sansonne, maps are provided showing the location of motifs painted by van Gogh, including Daubigny's garden, Dr. Gachet's garden, the café where he roomed, and the wheat field where he shot himself.

VAN GOGH'S WALK, SAINT-RÉMY, PROVENCE

At the office of tourism, place Jaures, maps are available showing locations where van Gogh painted his most famous motifs, including the asylum garden.

VAN GOGH'S WALK, SAINTES-MARIES-DE-LA-MER, CAMARGUE

At the office of tourism, rue Van Gogh, an information office provides directions to locations where van Gogh painted motifs, including the street of thatched cottages in his painting Street in Saintes-Maries *(1888) and the lavender field in his painting* View of Saintes-Maries *(1888) (now a parking lot). Though the street of thatched cottages no longer survives, numerous other thatched cottages in Saintes-Maries are available for holiday rental.*

Holland

KRÖLLER-MÜLLER STATE MUSEUM

Apeldoornseweg 250
7351 TA, Otterlo
Tel: 08382 1041
Significant collection of van Gogh's work set in a beautiful park.

VAN GOGH MUSEUM

Stadhouderskade 42
1071 ZD, Amsterdam
Tel: 020 67 32 121
Largest collection of van Gogh paintings in the world.

United States

CEDARIDGE FARM

Box 1, Gardenville, PA 18926
Tel: (215) 766-0699
Location of 20 theme gardens inspired by the letters and paintings of van Gogh, the garden spaces designed by Derek Fell and Carolyn Fell. Visits by appointment only.

bibliography

The body of scholarly work devoted to the life and art of Vincent van Gogh is immense. The following works are especially useful. *The Complete Letters of Vincent van Gogh,* although a monumental read (at three volumes of fine print), is well worth reading cover to cover, especially the third volume, containing the correspondence with his sister Wilhelmien (Wil) and sister-in-law Johanna (Jo). Irving Stone's bestselling *Dear Theo* is a selection of van Gogh's most poignant letters to his brother, reduced to 480 pages and available in a paperback edition.

Bernard, Bruce. *Vincent by Himself.* Boston: Bulfinch Press, 1985.

———. *Eyewitness Art: Van Gogh.* London: Dorling Kindersley, 1992.

Bumpus, Judith. *Van Gogh's Flowers.* London: Phaidon, 1989.

Husker, Jan. *The Complete Van Gogh: Paintings, Drawings, Sketches.* New York: Abrams, 1980.

Maurer, Naomi. *The Pursuit of Spiritual Wisdom: The Thought and Art of Vincent van Gogh and Paul Gauguin.* Madison, NJ: Fairleigh Dickinson University Press, 1998.

Stone, Irving. *Dear Theo: The Autobiography of Vincent van Gogh.* New York: Plume, 1995.

Van Gogh, Vincent. *The Complete Letters of Vincent van Gogh* (3 volumes). Boston: Bulfinch Press, 2000.

———. *The Letters of Vincent van Gogh.* Edited by Ronald De Leeuw. New York: Penguin Books, 1998.

———. *The Letters of Vincent van Gogh.* Edited and introduced by Mark Roskill. New York: Touchstone, 1997.

Walther, Ingo F., and Metzger Rainer. *Vincent van Gogh: The Complete Paintings.* Cologne: Taschen, 1990.

index